PROPHETIC
COMPANY

PROPHETIC COMPANY

the joyful journey toward building prophetic community

DAN MCCOLLAM

Published by:
SOUNDS OF THE NATIONS
6391 Leisure Town Road
Vacaville, CA 95687

Cover design: Shelby Gibbs, shelbygibbsgraphicdesign.com
Editing and interior design: Carol Cantrell, Regina McCollam

Printed in the USA

ISBN-13: 978-1535005425
ISBN-10: 1535005424

Dan McCollam's book *Prophetic Company* is a necessity for individuals, churches, and businesses that want to function in a healthy outpouring of prophecy. This book goes beyond just teaching on the subject. It has a strong biblical foundation, stories, and practical activations that make it come alive.

Get ready to go into the deep end of the Spirit. As Dan says in this book, "So, here we are, standing ankle deep in the waters of the greatest prophetic movement in history." Dive into this book and let it refresh and prepare you for more!

—Doug Addison
Author of *Understand Your Dreams Now* and *Personal Development God's Way,* DougAddison.com

Dan McCollam has been a dear friend of mine for nearly two decades. He is a father in the Lord who relentlessly pursues the Kingdom and His presence. Dano hits the bull's-eye with his new book *Prophetic Company*. With practical insight on training prophetic communities, Dano's wisdom and experience make this book a must-have for anyone longing to increase the effectiveness of the prophetic ministry in his or her church. This book could be a catalyst to prophetic transition that could launch our communities into a great adventure with God. I highly recommend this book!

—Kris Vallotton
Senior Associate Leader, Bethel Church, Redding, California
Co-Founder of Bethel School of Supernatural Ministry
Author of nineteen books, including *The Supernatural Ways of Royalty* and *Spirit Wars*

Prophetic Company fills the historical gaps and frames a future landscape for prophetic ministry. Prophets tend to be birthed in solitude but maturity comes only in community. Dano McCollam is a great teacher on the topic of prophecy as a lifestyle. *Prophetic Company* is a book that every church leader and every Christian should read. It is more than a prophetic perspective on what might be. It invites the reader to enter into an experience of a real-life company of prophets. I highly recommend it!

—Bob Hazlett
Speaker / Author of *The Roar: God's Sound in a Raging World*

Dan McCollam's new book *Prophetic Company* is easily the most unique book on the prophetic I have read in ten years. Dan's book threw open the curtains of my mind and allowed me to see things from a perspective I had never considered. I can't wait to see the effects of this teaching impact the Body of Christ worldwide. It's time for the Prophetic Movement 2.0!

—Dr. Jonathan Welton
Best-selling author & President of Welton Academy

Over the course of the 15 years that I have known and become a friend of Dan McCollam, I have come to realize that he carries one of the most amazing abilities to articulate Kingdom truths. In this book *Prophetic Community,* Dano brilliantly expresses what I have personally witnessed him successfully and diligently birth and build, a company of prophetic people. You will find many enlightening keys and breakthroughs for your own prophetic journey in this strategic and timely book.

Thanks, Dano, for your pioneering work!

—Keith Ferrante
Founder of Emerging Prophets
Author of *There Must Be More, Reforming the Church: From a House to a Home,* and *Restoring the Father's Heart*

Prophetic Company is another great example of Dano's watchword that every believer be "on the red-hot burning pursuit of biblical Christianity."

Prophetic Company is a biblical and historical study revealing the dream of God's heart that every son or daughter would truly know the heart, the mind, and the thoughts of their heavenly Father. Dan describes the different faces of the prophetic and how we can discover our individual and corporate identity as sons and daughters. Prophecy is a life skill to serve others, our community, our government, and the nations, and every believer has a valued contribution.

—Tammy Hawkins
Prophetic intercession and presbytery leader at The Mission in Vacaville, California
Author of *Partnering With Heaven: Praying For Your Children*

Table of Contents

Dedication

It seems appropriate in this book to have a longer dedication page recognizing the cherished prophetic influences from my past and the inspiring prophetic innovators of my current prophetic community.

In dedication to my first prophetic influences:

- To Cleddie Keith of Heritage Fellowship in Florence, Kentucky, my long-time pastor, mentor, and spiritual father. Thank you for starting my prophetic journey by modeling a life of asking, "What does the Lord say?"
- To Chuck and Myra Payne who taught me how to stir up the gift of God within me.

In dedication to the prophetic trainers who have served at The Mission in Vacaville, California, in years past:

- To Graham Cooke who brought me the challenge and subject of pursuing a prophetic company.
- To Byron and Crystal Easterling who taught me the importance of prophetic processing.
- To Joyce Milton, one of the most creative prophetic trainers I have ever met.
- To Dena McClure who modeled the love of the secret places of the Most High.

In dedication to my son, Michael, who taught me that seeing in the Spirit is a real thing.

- To Nathan, Jordan, and Tambre, my other children who continue the prophetic legacy.

In dedication to the influence of prophetic fathers:

- To Kris Vallotton who is a true prophet and a true friend. He has shaped my life with his love, counsel, and wisdom. I'm so grateful to God for you.

- To James Goll for calling out the prophetic office in me and modeling the life of a joy-filled prophet.

In dedication to current prophetic innovators in my circle of friends:

- To all the coaches and team members who serve at The Mission in Vacaville, California, whose faithful pursuit of prophetic company will be an inspiration for generations to come.

- To Josh and Cherie Cawley, dear friends, prophets, and partners in building the love and family connection within a prophetic community.

- To Ramon Santos for helping us make seers and mystics at home in the Body of Christ.

- To Mark and Tammy Hawkins for the gifts and graces they bring to prophetic intercessors and for their transformational impact as prophetic presbyters and servants to The Mission's 120 cities.

- To Keith and Heather Ferrante for advancing emerging prophets to the next level.

In dedication to the apostolic leaders in my life:

- To David and Deborah Crone for creating a nest for the eagles to land and a true and solid foundation for building prophetic company. I love and cherish your friendship, leadership, and counsel.

- To Bill Johnson for showing us all how to live from heaven to earth.

To the editorial team:

- To Carol Cantrell, my chief content editor and encourager.
- To Shelby Gibbs for her prophetic creativity in cover design.
- To Regina, my wife, my love, my strongest advancer and toughest editor.

This book is a representation of what I have learned from walking in the love and wisdom of prophetic community with all of you. Thank you.

1

Is Prophetic Company Biblical?

Honestly, the thought of creating a prophetic culture never crossed my mind before a friend asked me a very intriguing question. The query didn't arrive during a business meeting or strategic planning session; it popped up during a casual conversation at a local coffee shop. Graham Cooke, a seasoned veteran prophet, leaned over the table and asked, "Dano, are we a prophetic company, or do we just love prophecy?"

I pondered the question for a few moments. *I do love prophecy*, I reasoned. Understand that I had spent the first decade and a half of my Christian experience bored for the Lord in a cessationist background that never even mentioned the possibility of contemporary prophets or prophecy. When I discovered that God communicates His heart, His mind, and His intentions to humanity, it arrived as an earth-shaking revelation. I came alive discovering the personal attention God applies to each individual and the access each believer has to the thought life of the greatest genius in the universe. The spiritual awakening of the entire supernatural realm rose as just the spice of life I needed to begin the grand adventure of truly pursuing and discerning the voice of God. So, *Yes,* I reasoned internally, *I do love prophecy.*

Furthermore, I didn't know if I knew what a prophetic company was. How could I weigh the benefits of something I had no prior knowledge of? Realizing I hadn't answered him yet, I looked up from my thoughts and my half-empty glass of Mango Sunrise iced tea and asked, "I don't know, what's the difference?"

Then Graham, in his cryptic Gandalf-like way, answered, "Well, that would be a great one-year conversation with Holy Spirit. Wouldn't it?"

To be transparent with you, I walked away thinking, *Man, I hate it when he does that—answering a question with another question.* Still, that prophetic conundrum tormented me long after my friend had relocated to another part of the state.

Where Is Prophetic Company Found?

What is a prophetic company, and where is it found? The question threw me back into the well-worn pages of my faithful friend, the Bible. I found the term "company of the prophets" directly mentioned ten times in the Bible. "Company" comes from the Hebrew word *ben*,[1] meaning "sons, youth, or grandsons, or members of a group, guild, order, or class." The literal references to a "company of prophets" spoke directly to the ninth century BCE time period during the ministry of the prophets Elijah and Elisha as found in the following passages:

- 1 Kings 20:35 – first mention of the literal company of the prophets.

- 2 Kings 2:3, 5, 7, 15 – the transfer of company leadership from Elijah to Elisha.

- 2 Kings 4:1 – a reference to the wife of a man from the company of the prophets.

- 2 Kings 4:38 – a miracle performed amidst the company of the prophets.

---

[1] *Strong's Concordance,* #H1121.

- 2 Kings 5:22 – a reference to Gehazi lying to Naaman about the company of the prophets.

- 2 Kings 6:1 – the company of the prophets had outgrown their meeting place.

- 2 Kings 9:1 – Elisha commissions an assignment for one of the company.

It's clear from these passages that there is definite biblical ground for the concept of a prophetic company. It should be noted that prophetic community may have been made possible through the benevolence of Obadiah, who hid one hundred prophets in two caves while the evil Queen Jezebel was on a religious killing spree.[2]

Moses Foreshadows Prophetic Company

The idea of prophetic company, however, did not originate with the prophets Elijah and Elisha. I believe this heart for a prophetic company surfaced at least five hundred years earlier in the heart of Moses. Let's pick up the account in the book of Numbers.

> *So Moses went out and told the people what the* LORD *had said. He brought together seventy of their elders and had them stand around the tent. Then the* LORD *came down in the cloud and spoke with him, and he took some of the power of the Spirit that was on him and put it on the seventy elders. When the Spirit rested on them, they prophesied—but did not do so again. However, two men, whose names were Eldad and Medad, had remained in the camp. They were listed among the elders, but did not go out to the tent. Yet the Spirit also rested on them, and they prophesied in the camp. A young man ran and told Moses, "Eldad and Medad are prophesying in the camp." Joshua*

---

[2] 1 Kings 18:2-13.

son of Nun, who had been Moses' aide since youth, spoke up and said, "Moses, my lord, stop them!" But Moses replied, "Are you jealous for my sake? I wish that all the LORD's people were prophets and that the LORD would put his Spirit on them!"

11:24-29

Far from protecting his exclusive position as a prophet to the nation, Moses imparted prophetic grace and wished to live in the reality of a prophetic community.

The First Prophetic Company

The first recorded prophetic company (though not always referred to as that in Scripture) surfaced as early as the twelfth century BCE during the life of Samuel. At the beginning of his days we hear the sad commentary,

The boy Samuel ministered before the LORD under Eli. In those days the word of the LORD was rare; there were not many visions.

1 Samuel 3:1

Like many of us in the contemporary church, Samuel grew up in a time when prophetic utterances and experiences were rare.

Yet later in Samuel's lifetime, we see a whole procession of prophets coming down from the Philistine outpost, prophesying on instruments and creating a prophetic atmosphere that transformed the life and destiny of young Saul.[3] Still later in Scripture during the life of David, we see an assembly of prophets "prophesying with Samuel standing there as their leader."[4]

---

[3]   1 Sam. 10:5-11.

[4]   1 Sam.19:19-24.

It would appear that Samuel in his lifetime took the prophetic from a rare and individualistic expression to a prophetic company, that created far-reaching atmospheres of supernatural encounter and impact through the shared development of prophetic grace.

David Grasps the Value of a Prophetic Company

David perhaps saw the power created through the prophetic atmosphere modeled by Samuel and the company of prophets at Naioth. So together with the commanders of the army, David appointed a twenty-four-hour prophetic worship community.[5] I find it interesting that it was the commanders of the army, or we might say "The Department of Defense," that initiated the establishment of a prophetic worship community.

In addition to prophetic artists and musicians, David surrounded himself with prophetic counselors like Nathan and Gad.[6] It appears that prophetic community had become the new normal by 1,000 BCE. During this time, intentional prophetic community contributed to an unparalleled level of spiritual and physical prosperity in Israel's history as a nation.

New Testament Examples of Prophetic Company

Prophetic companies were not limited to the pages of the Old Testament. After AD 35, we see a group of prophets coming down from Jerusalem to Antioch.[7] Later in the book of Acts, we are informed that the church at Antioch had prophets and teachers: Barnabas, Simeon called Niger, Lucius of Cyrene, Manaean (who had been brought up with Herod the tetrarch), and Saul. This group of five first century Holy Ghost champions could certainly qualify as a prophetic company.

By AD 55, the prophetic gifts and graces had become so common

---

[5] See 1 Chron. 25.

[6] 1 Chron. 29:29.

[7] Acts 11:27.

in the early church that the Corinthian fellowship was given the instructions, "Two or three prophets should speak, and the others should weigh carefully what is said."[8] Think about the practical ramifications of this instruction. When you have so many prophets in your church that you must limit the prophetic utterances of prophets to two or three per service, then we must ask, "How many prophets do you have in this church?"

Further protocol is established in this verse as Paul continues to instruct, "Let the rest judge." In other words, the Corinthian church made provision and established protocols for how a company of prophets would operate within the context of a corporate service.

Conclusions

The weight of this biblical evidence caused me to consider the realities of prophetic companies much more seriously. It's clear in Scripture that prophetic companies have often existed. Yet, if this was the healthy norm in both the Old and New Testaments, what happened to prophetic gifts, graces, and the formation of prophetic communities? I will share what I discovered in answer to that question in our next chapter.

---

[8] 1 Cor. 14:29.

2

The Historical Veracity of the Prophetic

Having lived for decades in the church, I've seen many trends and fads pass through. Some of these spiritual stirrings are the rebuilding and restoration of lost eternal truths. The general resurgence of prophecy and the prophetic has only been common in the church for a little over one hundred years. With that relatively short blip on the monitor screen of millenniums of church history, how do we know this prophetic movement and the formulation of prophetic company is not just another passing fad or charismatic craze? If prophecy is so important, what happened to it? Why did it disappear in church history for so long? How biblical is the pursuit of prophecy? How needed is it if we don't see it alive in the history of the church?

Let's start by examining the occurrences of prophets and prophecy in Scripture. According to J. Barton Payne's *Encyclopedia of Biblical Prophecy*, there are 31,124 verses in the Bible. Of those thousands of Spirit-inspired utterances, 8,352 verses are future predictions. That means that 27 percent of the Bible is future prophetic predictions. Certainly, when you consider the actual prophetic content of the Bible, prophecy is more than a fad.

Etymology is the study of word origins and how word meanings change throughout history. Word studies serve as helpful keys for understanding biblical truths that were written in a different time period and language. So, to better understand the importance of prophets in Scripture, let's do a basic comparative word study.

There are at least seven different words used in the original language of the Bible that refer to a prophet or types of prophetic ministry. If we were to take the most prominent word for prophet in the Old Testament, *nabiy*,[9] and analyze its frequency in Scripture, we would find it listed 316 times. Then we could take the New Testament counterpart to this word, which is *prophetes*,[10] and discover that it appears 149 times. Add those two numbers together and you could formulate a very conservative total of 465 occurrences of the word "prophet" in Scripture.

Now, let's compare the role of prophet by frequency of usage to the other gift offices listed in Ephesians 4:11. By comparison, the words "pastor" and "shepherd" appear 191 times, "teacher" occurs only 162 times, "apostle(s)" is mentioned a mere 80 times, and "evangelist(s)" is surprisingly only directly mentioned by name three times. Once again, let's total up the usage of these four of the five ministry offices for a total of 436 direct references. To contrast and compare, "prophet" is mentioned more in the Bible than all the other five-fold gifts put together.

Add to this word study the fact that at least twelve individuals were called prophets in the New Testament:

- Agabus[11]
- Judas and Silas[12]
- The four virgin daughters of Philip the evangelist[13]

---

[9] *Strong's Concordance*, #H5030.
[10] *Strong's Concordance,* #G4396.
[11] Acts 11:27-28; 21:10-11.
[12] Acts 15:32.
[13] Acts 21:8-9.

- At least two of the men listed as prophets and teachers in Antioch.[14]

- The group of unnamed prophets that accompanied Agabus to Antioch.[15]

I'm not trying to exalt the gift of prophet above other important office gifts within the church, but it certainly begs the question, "What happened to the office of prophet?"

Prophecy in the Lists of Spiritual Gifts

Most Christians are familiar with the nine manifestation gifts of the Spirit listed in 1 Corinthians 12:8-10. I was surprised in my research to discover that some scholars propose as many as eight lists of spiritual gifts in the New Testament. The following passages comprise the eight proposed lists of spiritual gifts to which these scholars refer:

- Romans 12:6-8

- 1 Corinthians 12:8-10

- 1 Corinthians 12:28

- 1 Corinthians 12:29-30

- 1 Corinthians 13:1-3

- 1 Corinthians 14:26

- Ephesians 4:11

- 1 Peter 4:10-11

Whether we agree with the designation of these eight passages as gifts of the Spirit or not, it is interesting to note that the gift of prophecy (or prophet) is the only one to appear in every one of these lists. Historical Bible scholars also note that prophecy occurred in at least fourteen of the local churches mentioned in the New Testament.

---

[14] Acts 13:1.
[15] Acts 11:27.

Ernest Gentile, in his classic book, *Your Sons and Daughters Shall Prophesy: Prophetic Gifts in Ministry Today*, says of prophecy that it is the—

- most mentioned gift in the Bible lists.

- most explained gift in Scripture.

- most edifying to the whole church.

- most revealing of God's will.

- most available to all believers.

- most used gift by the Spirit in Scripture.

- most promoted of the spiritual gifts in Scripture.

- most connected gift with the person and ministry of Jesus Christ.

Prophecy in the Early Church

Beyond the biblical emphasis of prophets and prophecy, there are hundreds of historical references in the early church writings regarding prophecy. One such manuscript, *The Teaching of the Twelve*, is an early church manual that was widely circulated from AD 50-120. *The Didache,* as it is also called, contains four chapters[16] on how to receive traveling prophets. Our cessationist friends who believe that prophecy passed away with the completion of the biblical canon should note that the church was still receiving prophets after the last verse of Scripture was penned.

Ireneaus was the pupil of Polycarp, who was the disciple of John. Those are pretty impressive credentials. In AD 180, Ireneaus released a book, *Against Heresies*, doctrinally challenging the greatest lies in the church of his day. Here is a direct translation from chapter four of his book.

---

[16] Chapters 11-15.

Those who are in truth His disciples, receiving grace from Him, do in His name perform (miracles), so as to promote the welfare of other men, according to the gift which each one has received from Him. For some do certainly and truly drive out devils, so that those who have thus been cleansed from evil spirits frequently both believe (in Christ), and join themselves to the Church. Others have foreknowledge of things to come: they see visions, and utter prophetic expressions. Others still, heal the sick by laying their hands upon them, and they are made whole. Yea, moreover, as I have said, the dead even have been raised up, and remained among us for many years. . . . The name of our Lord Jesus Christ even now confers benefits (upon men), and cures thoroughly and effectively all who anywhere believe on Him.

So we see that foreknowledge of things to come, visions, and prophetic expressions were common in the church of the second century. In the third century, Cyprian of Carthage described in his ninth epistle a season where very young children were having ecstatic prophetic experiences in their church. The children, who couldn't even read yet, were describing heavenly scenes right out of the Bible in great detail with the biblical accuracy of a seasoned student of the Word. Cyprian wrote:

For besides the visions of the night, by day also, the innocent age of boys is among us filled with the Holy Spirit, seeing in an ecstasy with their eyes, and hearing and speaking those things whereby the LORD condescends to warn and instruct us . . .

For the first three centuries of church history, the gift of prophets and prophecy were fairly common in healthy spiritual communities.

Abuses and Atrophy

Throughout revival history, abuses, doctrinal errors, and misapplications appear in even the healthiest of spiritual environments. This truth is evidenced by the fact that Paul the Apostle dealt with many errors and abuses during the liveliest time of early church history. By the later half of the second century, complaints arose against a group referred to as the New Prophecy movement. Later they were labeled as Montanists after one of their founders Montanus. The practitioners of New Prophecy often seemed out of control, as if they were suddenly possessed by God. Though prophecy was still considered common in the second century, the ecstatic or trance-like state that the Montanists often prophesied from was no longer the normal custom of the church.

As one who has personally had some ecstatic spiritual experiences, I can't judge eighteen centuries later the genuineness of what this group experienced. Their spiritual zeal and discipline was admired by many spiritual fathers of the time, including Tertullian. Yet, because the passion of some churches and church leaders grew cold, the Montanists refused to have their prophecies judged by the clergy of their day. This refusal of biblical protocol to judge prophecy eventually led to some malpractices and doctrinal errors. Whenever prophetic declarations and manifestations are considered beyond judgment, then there is no opportunity for correction, improvement, or realignment for those who "prophesy in part."[17] Prophetic companies must remain accountable and teachable. These extreme practices and lack of proper protocol led some churches and church leaders to reject prophecy altogether.

By AD 260, the church began challenging the concept of universal grace and authority. Clergy started replacing the concept of universal grace with individual grace. In other words, they claimed that special people like bishops had the authority to prophesy and interpret Scripture but not the common man. When gifts of the Spirit become possible but not probable, they tend to atrophy. The dictionary definition of atrophy is "to decline in effectiveness or vigor due to underuse or neglect."

---

[17] 1 Cor. 13:9.

The word is originally derived from the Greek compound *a-* meaning "without" and *-trophe* meaning "food." When prophecy atrophies, it is for lack of food. Scripture clearly and repeatedly warns against this trend.

> *Do not neglect your gift, which was given you through prophecy when the body of elders laid their hands on you.*
>
> 1 Timothy 4:14

> *For this reason I remind you to fan into flame the gift of God, which is in you through the laying on of my hands.*
>
> 2 Timothy 1:6

> *Do not quench the Spirit. Do not treat prophecies with contempt but test them all; hold on to what is good, reject every kind of evil."*
>
> 1 Thessalonians 5:19-22

As charismatic zeal and practice became more controversial, religion turned more rational and less experiential. Growth started centering around Romans 12 gifts of organizational efficiency, which now trumped the early church manifestation gifts of 1 Corinthians 12. The spiritual climate began evolving from manifestations of presence and power to managerial expertise. The personal charisma of individual leadership began replacing the spiritual charismata at work in the whole congregation.

Conclusions

Both sides of the argument participated in the error that led to generations of prophetic erosion. The prophetically zealous refused to have their prophecies judged while others refused to stir up their God-given gifts. Spiritual abuses by the zealous minority coupled with the spiritual atrophy of the calloused majority practically erased the visible effects of the outpouring of Pentecost. The church essentially returned to Mount Sinai to once again reject the priesthood of all believers. They subtly reversed and rejected the Spirit being poured out on "all flesh" and relinquished their inheritance as a nation of priests and kings to a select few. This led to four false beliefs that paralyzed the majority of the church from experiencing the supernatural for centuries to come. We will examine these toxic lies in the next chapter.

3

Four Lies That Paralyze

Throughout the Synoptic Gospels, Jesus warned His disciples against three toxic types of philosophical yeast. The three cautions were described as the yeast of Herod, the yeast of the Pharisees, and the yeast of the Sadducees. In the book of Matthew, Jesus clearly explains that the word "yeast" refers to the teachings or practices of these various groups.[18] He directly defines the yeast of the Pharisees as hypocrisy.[19] The yeast of Herod could arguably be defined as a political spirit or compromise for the sake of position. But what is the meaning of the yeast of the Sadducees?

If Jesus said that the yeast was the contaminate qualities of each group's lives and teachings, then we should examine what the Sadducees taught. The book of Acts gives us the clearest summation of the Sadducees' teaching:

> *(The Sadducees say that there is no resurrection, and that there are neither angels nor spirits, but the*

---

[18] See Matt. 16:12.
[19] Luke 12:1.

Pharisees believe all these things.)

Acts 23:8

Sadducees denied the possibility of interaction with a spiritual realm. They centered only on a literal interpretation of the Scripture and the hope of a future physical empire.

Why Are the Sadducees of Interest?

Unfortunately, the conflicts within the church described in the last chapter led to a yeast of the Sadducees being kneaded into the mix of Christian theology for the following 1,800 years. The church became somewhat "pneumaphobic," that is, afraid to acknowledge or embrace any real possibility of contact with a spiritual world or realm beyond a sheer act of God's sovereignty. Many church movements formed or embraced an unspoken new trinity of Father, Son, and the Holy Bible, replacing the presence and activity of the Holy Spirit with a zeal for doctrinal uniformity. These trends in Christian thought left the idea of forming a prophetic company as complete heresy or spiritual fantasy. Though Christian thought is changing in wonderful ways, the yeast of the Sadducees is still alive and well in many churches of our day.

From the fading glory of the first three centuries of supernatural community, four false beliefs emerged that paralyzed the possibility of prophetic companies. Those beliefs I name as Cessationism, Exceptionism, Monasticism, and Vilification. Now, lest it appear that I am taking this space to criticize others in the following exposé, let me remind you and confess that I have personally lived with each one of these lies in my own life. I don't come as one pointing the finger but as one pointing the way out of these four paralyzing lies.

Cessationism

In Christianity, Cessationism is the belief that spiritual gifts such as speaking in tongues, prophecy, and healing, ceased with the original twelve apostles. Cessationists are divided into two basic camps: principled and empirical. Principled cessationists believe it is impossible for gifts of the Spirit to operate today because they were only used during the time of the apostles to verify their teaching until the Bible was completed. They believe the church can be perfectly guided to reach right decisions today if it only applies the principles, teachings, and examples of the Bible.

While I agree that a right interpretation of the Bible is the ultimate source for right decisions and an important part of every believer's life, the belief that we depend on the Bible above the Spirit of God sounds suspiciously similar to the yeast of the Sadducees who replaced any spiritual interaction with their own interpretation of Scripture. I contend that the Book (the Bible) points to the Author (Holy Spirit), not the Author to the Book.

Jesus didn't say, "Don't be sad that I am leaving, for I will give you a book." He said,

> *Unless I go away, the Advocate will not come to you: but if I go, I will send him to you . . . But when he, the Spirit of truth, comes, he will guide you into all the truth . . .*

> John 16:7, 13

Cessationist teaching may have begun as early as the third century. During that period, Origen Adamanius, one of the first systematic expositors of Christian theology, wrote that signs of the Apostolic Age were temporary and that no contemporary Christian exercised any of these early sign gifts. Yet, Origen himself professed to have been an eyewitness to instances of healing, exorcism, and prophecy though he refused to record the details lest he should "rouse the laughter of the unbeliever."[20] How can we take seriously the doctrinal viewpoints

---

[20]   Origen Adamantius. *Contra Celsum*, I, ii; III, xxiv; VII, iv, lxvii.

on spiritual gifts of someone who denies the foundation of their own experiences based on peer pressure and the fear of man? Though Origen certainly has credible contributions to the faith, we cannot consider him a credible source on the issue of spiritual gifts. We can, however, see that the ecclesiastical pressure to deny spiritual gifts was already in play by the third century.

The second type of Cessationism is the empirical. Empirical cessationists base their beliefs on experience. Their denial of the continuation of the gifts is based on their historical study of early church practices: "the charismatic gifts did indeed decline and were eventually lost sometime between the second and fourth centuries AD."[21]

John Chrysostom, Archbishop of Constantinople, was an important early church father who wrote in the early fifth century on 1 Corinthians 14 and the discussion of the gift of tongues:

> *This whole place is very obscure; but the obscurity is produced by our ignorance of the facts referred to and by their cessation, being such as then used to occur but now no longer take place. And why do they not happen now? Why look now, the cause too of the obscurity hath produced us again another question: namely, why did they then happen, and now do so no more?*[22]

Cessationists are often great Christians with a genuine relationship with God and a zeal for biblical truth. Such was the theological atmosphere I was raised in. However, I must admit that there are a lot of problems with Cessationism. The teachings of Cessationism are neither biblically nor historically sound. Scripture does not teach that the gifts will cease with the completion of the Bible. One also cannot say that gifts ceased with the finishing of the Bible if you have already acknowledged that they existed up to the fourth century. In fact, you

---

[21] biblestudy.net, *Preliminary Proof: When the Gifts Would Cease.*

[22] "FathChrysHomXXIX". Piney.com, "cessationism".

can trace the moving of the Holy Spirit and operation of the gifts of the Spirit in every generation since the original twelve apostles if you are only willing to look. Though the church at large rejected these gifts by the third and fourth centuries, you can in no way infer from this general negligence of the gifts that they somehow no longer existed or were no longer available. Cessationism is merely a lie propagated by a myth of extinction. Scripture repeatedly warns us to beware of these types of lies that deny the truths of God for the myths of modern opinion.[23]

Exceptionism

Okay, I'll be quite honest here. "Exceptionism" is a word I created to define a documented historic belief—the word is a neologism, and you won't find it on your spell checker or anywhere in a Bible dictionary. Since I made up the word, it is also my obligation to define it. Exceptionism as I am applying it refers to the belief that God can still do miracles through exceptional people or in exceptional circumstances, but it is not His normal mode of operation. It is basically the rejection of universal grace that I spoke of in the last chapter.

As we already noted, by AD 260, many church leaders claimed that special people like bishops had the authority to prophesy and interpret Scripture but not the common man. This point became so strong in common thought that by AD 1,000, the official stance of the Roman Catholic Church, as published in the Roman Ritual (and quoted in Eddie L. Hyatt's *2000 Years of Charismatic Christianity*), stated:

> . . . *That speaking in tongues among the common people was to be considered* prima facie *(evidence that unless rebutted would be sufficient to prove a particular position or fact) evidence of demon possession. Among the monastic's and Church hierarchy however, it could be considered evidence of sainthood.*

---

[23] See 1 Tim. 1:4, 4:7; 2 Tim. 4:4; Titus 1:14.

There you have it. Special people can do special things, but you are not special. Do you realize how this eats at the very fabric of the gospel?

One of the things that confuses people is that the Old Testament does appear to function on a basis of Exceptionism. In its records, you have only a few special people doing special things throughout the centuries. But God came to this earth not only to forgive us but to also free us from the power of sin that He might fill us with the fullness of God. God's goal did not end with forgiveness but rather at fullness. God's desire and dream was to upgrade all flesh by filling everyone with His Holy Spirit so that every son and daughter could hear the voice of God. Exceptionism needed to be named and exposed because it attempts to rob the Good News of its essential goodness: access to the divine nature.

I sometimes wonder if the seven sons of Sceva were not victims of an Exceptionism lie. When they tried to cast out a demon, the spirit responded, "Jesus I know, and Paul I know, but who are you?" Then the demon-possessed man overpowered the seven sons and gave them such a beating that they ran out of the house naked and bleeding. I know that it is possible that these sons of a priest did not know Christ, but it seems to me that they were following the pattern they had seen and were giving honor to Jesus. Is it possible that the sons of Sceva knew who Christ was but didn't know who they were in Christ?

When you lose identity, you relinquish authority. When praying for the sick, I've often heard the enemy challenge me with something like, "Who do you think you are to do this? Do you think you are qualified for this? Are you spiritual enough to heal right now?" I know the answer now; but in my younger years, I often felt paralyzed and ineffective through an unhealthy practice of self-examination. I wondered if I were really spiritually qualified to do the stuff. Was I special enough?

Another form of Exceptionism suggests that God only moves in exceptional circumstances. For example, God might heal people where there are no doctors or medicines, but it wouldn't normally happen in civilized cultures. This belief implies that only extreme circumstances motivate the movement of God's sovereign hand. Wow! It almost sounds spiritual, yet this lie falsely suggests that first world cultures have somehow outgrown their need for God and the supernatural. The lie subtly suggests that education and social evolution have displaced the need for supernatural experience.

I am convinced that Jesus Christ died not only to make us special, but also because the Father already saw us all as special. He released new birth through the work of Christ and special abilities by the power of the Holy Spirit so that all believers can manifest the new birth as sons and daughters of God.

Exceptionism is a toxic denial of the love of God, the riches of His grace, and the power of the gospel. The revelation of God in Scripture demonstrates that He is not moved by exceptional need but rather by simple faith. Exceptionism is a lie that disqualifies believers from an essential part of their spiritual inheritance.

Monasticism

This one is a real word. Monasticism in itself is far from evil; but as a means of obtaining the supernatural, it tends to impoverish the riches of God's grace. Monasticism can be simply defined as "withdrawing from everyday life to concentrate on prayer and meditation." It is the rule or system of life in a monastery where religious observance, asceticism, austerity, non-indulgence, and self-denial are the means applied towards greater awareness of God. Again, there is nothing wrong with Monasticism or its way of life.

But in the third to fifth centuries AD, the church was growing stronger in its criticism of supernatural manifestations. Many of those whom we now call "the desert fathers" retreated from the established church to previously uninhabited territories to pursue their relationship with God, minister to the poor, and build communities based on biblical kingdom values. As a result, miracles were happening in the desert places much more frequently than in the average established church.

This contrast between the stale, controlling environment of the established church and the supernatural freedom and power of the desert church gave birth to another lie. The lie goes something like this: "If I could just get away from life, this world, and other people, I could be spiritually powerful."

A similar and much more controversial lie would suggest that the level of my spirituality is directly related to the proportion of my exercise of spiritual disciplines. This lie subtly implies that I can earn greater spiritual mastery through human effort and works. Paul takes this lie head-on in the book of Galatians.

> *You foolish Galatians! Who has bewitched you? Before your very eyes Jesus Christ was clearly portrayed as crucified. I would like to learn just one thing from you: Did you receive the Spirit by the works of the law, or by believing what you heard? Are you so foolish? After beginning by means of the Spirit, are you now trying to finish by means of the flesh? Have you experienced so much in vain—if it really was in vain? So again I ask, does God give you his Spirit and work miracles among you by the works of the law, or by your believing what you heard?*
>
> 3:1-5

Paul clearly shows here that miracles come through believing not achieving. It's true that you can **learn** greater spiritual mastery through spiritual disciplines, but you cannot **earn** it through performance. That difference is more than semantic; it is the demarcation line between law and grace. If a person could earn spiritual mastery through disciplines alone, then the Pharisees would have been the most powerful, spiritual people on earth.

The problem with this view of the desert fathers is that people tend to reverse the order of events. The desert fathers did not become spiritual because they went out to the desert; they went out to the desert because they were spiritual already. In other words, because of the stifling formalism of the established church and the persecution of religious freedom, the desert fathers sought a place of asylum where they could pursue the spirituality they already possessed.

Power in the supernatural comes by a radical act of God's grace accompanied by the faith response of risk taking. It's illogical for one to think that if he could just get away from people and society, he could then qualify to perform powerful spiritual acts. Who would they be performed on? The gifts of the Spirit are not merit badges to be earned; they are gifts given to vulnerable vessels and designed to bless people, cities, and nations. Separating ourselves from others does not in itself make us holy. How would we then practice the law of love? Spiritual disciplines are important, and time alone with God can increase our sensitivity, revelation, and awareness of what we have already been given through the riches of God's grace. However, when Monasticism is practiced or thought of as a qualifier for spiritual gifts, it is simply a lie.

Vilification

The final lie I wish to address is Vilification. To vilify is to attack the reputation of a person or thing with strong and abusive criticism. In the context of the supernatural, it means to attribute to Satan, self, or evil what actually comes from God. We saw this in the instance of the Roman Ritual, which said that if a priest spoke in tongues, it was a qualification for sainthood; but if a common person spoke in tongues, then it must be the devil or witchcraft.

The Roman Ritual account reminds us of the position the Pharisees took concerning the ministry of Jesus:

> *But when the Pharisees heard this, they said, "It is only by Beelzebul, the prince of demons, that this fellow drives out demons."*

> Matthew 12:24

Jesus warned His followers that this tactic of the enemy would accompany their supernatural ministry.

It is enough for students to be like their teachers, and servants like their masters. If the head of the house has been called Beelzebul, how much more the members of his household!

Matthew 10:25

I remember an extraordinary meeting early in my itinerant ministry. When I stepped up to speak for the first session of the meeting, hundreds of people were instantly slain in the Spirit. Prophetic words came forth, and many people were filled with the Holy Spirit. It was truly one of the strongest meetings I had ever been in up to that point. The next night the senior pastor stood up to introduce me and began to apologize to his congregation. He publicly denounced me and the manifestations of the Spirit that had happened the night before. "We will never have a speaker like this again," he promised. "From now on, we will only have safe speakers."

I flew home from that meeting so dejected. It's never my goal to hurt people or in any way be disruptive. I felt that I somehow must have done something wrong. For six months, I hung my head and battled feelings of insecurity and depression. Then, one night at my home church, a guest speaker called me out and gave me a word of wisdom, "Dano, the power of your anointing will increase in proportion to your ability to endure persecution." That was the entire word, and I will never forget it. I was flabbergasted. God spoke directly into my situation.

Though I don't believe there is any inherent virtue in being intentionally controversial, I did come to understand that conflict and criticism will either enlarge you or shrink you. People who don't understand the supernatural or don't have a theology that allows it, don't have many choices but to attribute unexplained works to the devil. We must choose to let criticism humbly enlarge our desire to serve God in truth and endure what comes with it.

All in all, these four lies contributed greatly to the diminishing presence of supernatural gifts and power in the church. As we learned, Cessationism claimed the gifts were no longer needed. Exceptionism made supernatural displays possible but not probable, and then only through special people or in extreme circumstances. The misplaced conclusions of outsiders caused Monasticism to hide grace gifts behind a religious performance façade, luring us into the lie that we must earn the supernatural power that we already have through relationship. Finally, Vilificationism accused those who did flow in spiritual gifts of a less than pure root.

Though history clearly demonstrates that there have always been spiritual gifts and prophetic graces in the church, centuries of compounded ignorance left the majority of the universal church without clear evidence of spiritual gifts, prophecy, or any form of prophetic company.

Lies in Subtle Forms

Even if you have never believed any of these lies as a matter of theology, you have probably wrestled with them in their more subtle forms. Perhaps you believe that gifts of the Spirit are certainly for today, but you have said something like, "Prophecy just isn't my gift." That's a form of personal Cessationism. Though we each have differing gifts, Scripture makes it clear that anyone can prophesy.

Or have you ever admired someone else's gift or grace so much that you spoke the words, "I could never be like that. I could never do what they are doing." Welcome to the subtle lie of Exceptionism.

I personally spent years in the lie of Monasticism, thinking I could earn power, gifts, revival, or presence through stronger exercise and devotion to spiritual discipline. Every time a need for a spiritual gift would arise, I would go into self-examination mode, "Am I qualified for this? Have I prayed enough? Loved enough? Read enough? Fasted enough?" The obvious answer was, "No. You can never do enough."

The internal religious lie screamed, "Do this, do that, do more, do, do, do . . ." In the end, I realized with Paul the Apostle that all my attempts at self-qualification were just that—"doo-doo" compared to the excellency of knowing Him.[24]

Furthermore, I realized that my struggle revealed the whole purpose of Christ's coming: I could never do enough, so Christ came and exchanged His righteousness for my spiritual inadequacies. He qualified me by grace through faith—and that not of my own; it is a gift from God—not by works, so that I cannot boast.[25] When someone walks up to me who is blind or has cancer and asks for prayer, I cannot afford to take an inward journey of self-analysis. I must step into the grace extended to me through the cross of Jesus Christ and step out in the measure of faith that He has given me to do the impossible.

But what of this final foe—Vilification? Not everyone will face the kind of public denunciation that I experienced in that large church, but most people will encounter this lie in its subtle form. Personal Vilification is the lie that responds to a prophetic impression or hearing God's voice with, "That's probably just me. This is my imagination. I'm deceiving myself." Unfortunately, most Christians try to live the new life under an old man, orphan mentality. We live with a spiritual default that says, "It's probably just me, but it possibly could be God." I realized that my personal default denied the glory of the cross and the Spirit's work of new creation.

Changing My Personal Default

To rid myself of the hideous monsters of self-qualification, self-analysis, and personal Vilification, I began to ask the following questions:

- If I gave my life to God, do I truly believe He took it?

- Did He give me a new heart?

- Do I have the mind of Christ?

---

[24] Phil. 3:8.
[25] Eph. 2:9, Gal. 2:16.

- Does His Spirit live in me?
- Will He ever leave me or forsake me?

If these things are true as Scripture says they are, then my default needs to be, "It's probably God, but it could be me." Looking to God first inclines me toward an active rather than a passive personal default mode. This position empowers me to not lean on my own understanding, but acknowledge Him in all my ways so that He can direct my life in a supernatural path.[26]

There is a spiritual principle that states, "You are currently moving at the speed of your own obedience." How many times does it take you to hear from God before you respond? Does it take three impressions, two Scriptures, a prophecy, and four confirmations? Then, that will be the speed of your growth. In this position, nothing will ever happen until you get all the data you need to step out. "But I just want to be sure," we all say defensively. The truth is, faith is based upon taking the risk and not always having all the answers. Personal Vilification keeps us in a double-minded state that makes us always fearful of stepping out.

Quenching Revival

The great Welsh revivalist, Evan Roberts, struggled with personal Vilification. In his early twenties, Evan played a key role in the 1904 Welsh Revival that swept over one hundred thousand people suddenly into the kingdom of God. The meetings Evan facilitated were characterized by seeking the Lord, spiritual freedom, and a spontaneous flow that allowed God to move in unprecedented ways. Unfortunately, Evan didn't take good care of his own physical and mental health.

With all the meetings and late nights of prayer, the young revivalist's body and mind just broke down. Evan had to stop the meetings and seek a place of physical and emotional rest.

---

26 Prov. 3:5-6.

After the breakdown, young Evan began to question whether he was truly hearing from God or not. He came under the influence of some teaching that claimed there was a desperate war raging between his soul and spirit and that only by the most careful observation could he truly be certain he was hearing from God. Evan's exhaustion, combined with this theological uncertainty, rendered the young revivalist powerless to discern the reliability of the impressions he received from the Holy Spirit. The revival died out in Wales, and Evan lived the rest of his life in seclusion, confused and largely ineffective.

This young powerhouse who had served as a catalyst for the Pentecostal revival of the twentieth century, faded into obscurity. Evan's story mirrors the history of the church. When we have more faith in the power of the devil to deceive us than the power of God to instruct us, then we have done for the devil what he could not do for himself. We have exalted his throne above the throne of God and made him like the Most High.[27]

I'm convinced that these four lies have robbed the church of her spiritual dominion for far too long. It's time for the church to rise and shake off the shabby shackles of Cessationism, Exceptionism, Monasticism, and Vilification and to run the race marked out for her by the Lord Jesus Christ. After all, it is impossible for us to be like Him and not manifest power.

Part of this awakening will be the formation of prophetic company and communities. In the following chapter, we will explore what I discovered to be the distinctive qualities of a prophetic company in our local community.

---

[27] Isa. 14:13.

4

Who Can Prophesy?

Once I understood some of the reasons why supernatural gifts and prophetic companies diminished historically, I felt confident and free to explore what a contemporary prophetic community might look like. The first distinctive I heard from the Holy Spirit and the witness of Scripture was:

A prophetic company is a people who believe everyone can prophesy.

What surprised me about this first distinctive of prophetic community is that it immediately contrasted what I had seen modeled in the church of the 1970s and 1980s. Upon leaving the empirical Cessationism of my denominational church, I quickly found myself in the company of people who called themselves Charismatics or Pentecostals. The gifts of the Spirit were not rare among these people but neither were they by any means perfect.

Most of the meetings I attended in Charismatic and Pentecostal circles were characterized by one or two older folks getting really excited whenever they perceived the moving of the Spirit. Suddenly, these lightning rods of religious zeal would jump up from their pew and yell a few ecstatic words in an unknown tongue. As the stream of spiritual babel subsided, there would often be a short pause where the congregation would wait for interpretation—a sort of holy calm after the storm. From the perspective of my previous religious background, this practice was both strange and wonderful; strange because it appeared that sometimes the same words could have different interpretations, and wonderful because at least people were stirring up gifts of the Spirit that my hungry inner man longed for.

When Prophets Come to Town

In those days, it seemed to me that prophecy was mostly available to us when a prophet came to town. Prophets came in many flavors and styles. Most of them followed the same unwritten format. They would gaze mysteriously across the congregation and then call out one or two "lucky" persons. Some people would try to hide themselves from the gaze of the prophet and others would stare them down. I even knew of people who dressed in certain bright colors hoping that it would attract the attention of a prophet so that they might receive a prophetic word.

The fortunate called-out ones would then stand and receive a public prophetic word. The rest of us would watch in awe, wonder, and sometimes terror as the word was being given. I remember thinking that prophets must see every fault I had and every unclean thing I ever thought. I would literally "plead the blood" of Jesus over myself when I knew a prophet was coming to town. My inner dialogue during those times went something like this, *Lord, I don't know of anything specific that I am doing to grieve You, but if there is anything—any sin in my life—please show it to me rather than the prophet so I can repent of it.* The funny thing is now I'm exactly the opposite. Now I think, *Lord, if there is anything that is a hindrance in my life, then please show me or someone else around me so that it can be dealt with.*

Our brand of the prophetic in those days seemed to be a mild form of Exceptionism mixed with Monasticism that implied that special people could do special things because they were so close to God. We in the congregation knew that we could somehow do the same things if we achieved the same level of spiritual sanctification. Unfortunately, that level of spiritual mastery seemed just beyond our reach.

God's Dream

As I pondered the distance between the distinctive that God was emphasizing and my personal experience, a Scripture came alive in my spirit. The text came from the ninth century BCE prophet Joel.

> *And it shall come to pass afterward that I will pour out My Spirit on all flesh; your sons and your daughters shall prophesy, your old men shall dream dreams, your young men shall see visions. And also on My menservants and on My maidservants I will pour out My Spirit in those days.*

> 2:28-29, NKJV

Joel's words expressed a dream from the very heart of God. God didn't just want one or two persons who could know His thoughts, His heart, and His words. God's dream for humanity is that every son and daughter could prophesy. My mentor used to say, "Dano, nothing gives a man more dignity than knowing he can hear the voice of God." That statement is so true. God desired to dignify humanity with sonship. He had it in His heart all along that one day through the atoning work of His Son, He could upgrade all flesh to a place of hearing, seeing, and perceiving by the outpouring of His Spirit.

A flood of revelation hit me. This is when I first came to understand that God didn't just come to forgive me of sin but to free from the power of sin so that He might ultimately fill me with the fullness of God. Sin stood as the obstacle between God and His dream for humanity. The goal, however, did not stop with the forgiveness of sin;

45

that was merely a means to an end. God's end objective transformed mankind into a nation of priests and kings. In the Old Covenant there were a few special people called prophets, priests, and kings; in the New Covenant, everyone is truly and uniquely special—"a nation of priests and kings."

> *But you are a chosen people, a royal priesthood, a holy nation, God's special possession, that you may declare the praises of him who called you out of darkness into his wonderful light.*
>
> 1 Peter 2:9

Paul Echoes God's Dream

Paul echoes God's dream and shows that it is very much alive in the heart of a New Testament church. For after clearly delineating that each person has unique spiritual gifts chosen and delivered by God, the apostle goes on to command all believers to desire greater gifts.

> *Now eagerly desire the greater gifts.*
>
> 1 Corinthians 12:31

Then again at the beginning of chapter fourteen, Paul exhorts us with greater detail:

> *Follow the way of love and eagerly desire gifts of the Spirit, especially prophecy. For anyone who speaks in a tongue does not speak to people but to God. Indeed, no one understands them; they utter mysteries by the Spirit. But the one who prophesies speaks to people for their strengthening, encouraging and comfort. Anyone who speaks in a tongue edifies themselves,*

but the one who prophesies edifies the church. I would like every one of you to speak in tongues, but I would rather have you prophesy . . .

1 Corinthians 14:1-5

Paul was expressing the heavenly Father's desire that all sons and daughters would prophesy. The difference is that eight hundred years after the writings of Joel, this dream became reality on the day of Pentecost with the outpouring of God's Spirit on all flesh. Now, truly, every son and daughter in the kingdom of God can—and should—prophesy!

Is Everyone a Prophet?

Many people ask at this point, "Dano, are you saying that everyone is a prophet?" Certainly not. The context of First Corinthians chapter twelve makes this very clear:

All are not apostles, are they? All are not prophets, are they? All are not teachers, are they? All are not workers of miracles, are they? All do not have gifts of healings, do they? All do not speak with tongues, do they? All do not interpret, do they? But earnestly desire the greater gifts.

vs. 29-31, NASB

While we see that everyone has differing primary gifts and that by our differences we experience a corporate synergy and value for one another based upon these specialties, the very end of the passage reminds us again that we are not limited to our current gift set but should eagerly desire greater gifts. However, the five-fold gifts of apostles, prophets, evangelists, pastors, and teachers seem to be appointed and called rather than pursued. Perhaps that is because the role of an office gift is so different from the purpose of a manifestation gift.

The gift of prophecy is available to everyone, and its purpose as we saw in 1 Corinthians 14 is to strengthen, encourage, and comfort. The office of a prophet is something that God calls, appoints, and chooses. The purpose of the gift that Christ gave in the form of the office prophet is revealed in the fourth chapter of the book written to the Ephesians.

> *So Christ himself gave the apostles, the prophets, the evangelists, the pastors and teachers, to equip his people for works of service, so that the body of Christ may be built up until we all reach unity in the faith and in the knowledge of the Son of God and become mature, attaining to the whole measure of the fullness of Christ.*
>
> 4:11-13

We can clearly see that the purpose of prophecy is to edify people, and the purpose of prophets is to equip the Body of Christ with prophetic grace. Far from a spirit of self-preservation and protecting their position from others, prophets dispense a grace for everyone to hear from God. This reminds us of a passage of Scripture we looked at in earlier chapters.

> *A young man ran and told Moses, "Eldad and Medad are prophesying in the camp." Joshua son of Nun, who had been Moses' aide since youth, spoke up and said, "Moses, my lord, stop them!" But Moses replied, "Are you jealous for my sake? I wish that all the LORD's people were prophets and that the LORD would put his Spirit on them!"*
>
> Numbers 11:27-29

Moses had it right; true prophets don't protect their position from others receiving prophetic grace for that is the very goal and purpose of the prophetic office itself.

True Prophets Create Prophetic Atmospheres

True prophets create prophetic atmospheres where it is easy for others to prophesy. Remember what happened to Saul, the son of Kish? He entered the presence of several prophets prophesying on their instruments, and the Spirit of God came powerfully upon Saul until he joined in their prophesying. The change was so drastic that those with Saul asked, "What is this that has happened to the son of Kish? Is Saul also among the prophets?" The story of Saul's prophetic encounter spread so rapidly through the land that this question actually became a saying in the time of Saul, "Is Saul also among the prophets?"[28]

The same type of encounter happens later in Naioth at Ramah. Saul had fallen out of favor with God through disobedience and sought to kill David. He heard that David was staying with the prophets at Naioth and sent men to capture him. Let's pick up the story in Scripture:

> *But when they saw a group of prophets prophesying, with Samuel standing there as their leader, the Spirit of God came on Saul's men, and they also prophesied. Saul was told about it, and he sent more men, and they prophesied too. Saul sent a third time, and they also prophesied . . . So Saul went to Naioth at Ramah. But the Spirit of God came even on him, and he walked along prophesying until he came to Naioth. He stripped off his garments, and he too prophesied in Samuel's presence. He lay naked all that day and all that night. This is why people say, "Is Saul also among the prophets?"*

> 1 Samuel 19:20-21, 23-24

---

[28] See 1 Sam. 10:8-13.

So we see several instances in Scripture where a prophetic atmosphere created by prophets released grace for others to prophesy. This is a biblical foreshadowing of the New Testament office of prophet.

Forming a Prophetic Company

Biblically, it seems that prophetic companies were made of people who were all called to the prophetic office. But what about the tabernacle of David? Could we call this a prophetic company? Here, musicians and singers were trained by the hundreds how to prophesy with their instruments and voices. This trained prophetic company became the singers and musicians present at the dedication of Solomon's temple when the glory of God filled the temple and overwhelmed everyone.

Let's stop a moment and gather the facts thus far. God desires that everyone prophesy. He poured out His Spirit on all flesh so that every son and daughter could prophesy. He still anoints and appoints the office prophet, who dispenses training and grace to make it even easier to prophesy. David may have formed an Old Testament prototype for a New Testament model of prophetic company. From these biblical observations, I began to dream about what a prophetic community could look like. What if a prophetic company was more than a round table of those holding the office of prophet? What if a prophetic company could include all of those trained in the gift of prophecy as well as prophets?

If a prophetic company is truly a group of people in which everyone can prophesy, then it must—by implication—include all those who prophesy. At my local church, The Mission in Vacaville, California, we recognize five unique spokes developing within our prophetic company that contribute to the weight and value of our prophetic community. I don't believe these delineations will fit every church's structure nor am I necessarily recommending them, but I would like to give further testimony to how this idea developed in our own culture.

The five spokes that each contribute unique strengths to our prophetic company are as follows:

- Team members
- Team coaches
- Seers and mystics
- Prophets
- Presbyters

I will share a little bit about each one of these spokes in the next few chapters so that you can become familiar with what I mean by each of these terms and what each distinction contributes to the prophetic company. My examples will mostly relate to the local church because that is my primary sphere of influence. I believe that every prophetic company should live in healthy connection with the local church, but the scope and impact of prophetic ministry should not be limited to local church. Please understand that by defining the spokes of my own prophetic company from the vantage point of the local church, I am in no way implying that they should be limited to that sphere, or that these are the only designations that should or could exist. I am merely speaking from the experience of my own joyful journey. With that said, let's further explore these five spokes of prophetic company.

5

Coaches and Team Members

Our prophetic company at The Mission did not start from a void. By 2010, I had spent twelve years serving and training under gifted prophetic fathers in the Greater Cincinnati area, followed by eleven years on the core leadership team of The Mission in Vacaville, California. The humble and empowering apostolic leadership of David and Deborah Crone at The Mission drew high-level resident prophets like Graham Cooke, Byron Easterling, Dena McClure, and Keith Ferrante as well as the fatherly influences of visiting prophets such as Ernest Gentile, James Goll, Dr. Mark Chironna, Bobby Conner, and others. In the early days of our school of the supernatural, we practiced daily training in the prophetic with Dena, Graham, and another gifted trainer, Joyce Milton.

I benefited greatly from the sharpening that came by associating with these amazing prophetic leaders. During that time and to the present, it has also been my great privilege to co-found the Bethel School of the Prophets with Kris Vallotton. Kris, among others, is a strong and valued prophetic voice into our house. He is a long-time friend and a true prophet in my personal life. I share all of this background information so that you understand that all of these prophetic influences created a healthy and robust spiritual atmosphere at The Mission.

Before we began forming a structured prophetic community, a rather organic and powerful prophetic atmosphere already existed. The Mission was even at that time the kind of place where you could tap just about anyone on the shoulder, ask for a prophetic word, and receive something both encouraging and accurate. In our case, structuring the community first came out of a recognition of what was already there.

The reader who is starting a prophetic culture from nothing or is only beginning the joyful journey has the advantage of defining and establishing common values and a healthy structure within their prophetic community right from the beginning. Within every church, there are people who are having prophetic perceptions, insights, and encounters; they may just lack context or language for it. As you begin biblical training and activation on prophecy and prophetic impressions (even if you must substitute the phrases "hearing God" or "encountering God" for more direct prophetic language), the potential within your own prophetic community will begin to surface.

Structure Rising from Necessity

The first two spokes of our prophetic company rose out of necessity. People were attending our services and conferences with an expectation of receiving prophetic ministry. Our usual mode of operation was for one of the core church leaders to send out a call for volunteers with two qualifications: they had some form of prophetic training and a willingness to prophesy. Next, we quickly threw these volunteers into a dozen or more teams who would minister in groups of two to four to those who had come to receive a word. This method worked great for a long time, and of course, we used evaluation forms to keep tabs on each team's accuracy and to reinforce the values of our prophetic protocol.

The problem at the end of the day was not in this method's effectiveness, but the trouble hearkened back to the question Graham had asked me years before, "Is this a prophetic community, or do we just love prophecy?" The danger threatening the concept of prophetic company lurked in the randomness of it all. Could we really call this community? What were the connection points beyond our shared ability to prophesy? Was a follow-up form really showing us what was going on in those prophetic appointments?

In my heart, I longed for more.

Team Members and Coaches

The answer for us came in the form of appointing coaches over every team. Coaches don't have to be the most prophetic person on their team; they just need to possess two things: good people skills and a clear understanding of the values and vision that form our prophetic protocol. Coaches are asked to choose two to eight team members whom they enjoy working with. These recruits become a permanent part of their prophetic team. We also encourage coaches to vary their team with beginner, intermediate, and advanced level team members. This little bit of structure produces multiple advantages.

The first advantage of this structure for leadership comes in the form of convenience. The method proves way easier. Leaders only need to call ten coaches rather than to recruit and organize one hundred volunteers. Each coach will call a few of their team members to find out who is available to minister within that particular week. People are busy. By having multiple team members who make up each potential team, the same volunteers are not over-taxed. By giving people more freedom in the scheduling and by having the same person call and recruit them for each prophetic opportunity, relationships and community grew.

We encourage coaches to be in regular contact with their team members in addition to the times of recruiting them for ministry opportunities. Coaches serve as a sort of pastor for prophetic teams. Some send texts or emails; others meet for coffee; some have home groups; others just hang out as the opportunities arise. There are no strict guidelines on how to connect with the team or how often coaches are required to meet with their teams, just a general encouragement to assist in the goal of growing and developing prophetic community through intentional relationships.

Building the Connection

In addition to the coaches, I appointed a couple who pastor the coaches, Josh and Cherie Cawley. This couple sends a weekly email to all of the prophetic coaches. They wisely vary the content of these emails. Some contain training information while others an encouraging word. Coach emails could also contain a testimony or an opportunity for ministry. Every week there is some form of connection through these emails. The Cawleys help with establishing new coaches, training them, and pastoring them through challenges.

I meet personally with all the coaches *en masse* about once a month. This meeting has many of the same elements as our emails. We share current testimonies of how our prophetic ministry is touching the lives of others, upcoming opportunities for ministry, coaching tips and advanced skills, and how to keep the greater vision in front of the larger prophetic community. This is a fun and encouraging time.

Coaches also play a key role in advancing the company by being aware of when their team members are ready to become coaches themselves. Coaches make the best recruiters because they personally observe both a candidate's people skills and prophetic accuracy in the target environment. By coaches multiplying themselves, the number of our teams can grow to meet the increasing need. We started our prophetic company with just three or four coaches and then grew to around twenty-five. Our goal is to raise up at least 50 coaches in the first few years to enable us to minister to 500 people in one sitting and then double again by raising up 100 coaches and teams that could serve 1,000 people.

Real-Time Coaching

To demonstrate the need for coaches, let me introduce you to a prophetic team member we will call Hannah Houseword. Hannah is the kind of person who gives the same basic prophetic word to everyone she meets. In Hannah's case, she prophesied to every third person or so that God was going to give them a house. The word Hannah gave people wasn't bad or unbiblical, but it seemed odd to hear the same word over and over again; God is not handing out free houses to every third person. We might not have caught that weakness with our old method of forming random volunteer teams and handing out evaluation forms at the end of the prophetic ministry time. People receiving prophetic ministry would not have questioned this word on their evaluation forms because everyone likes to hear that they will receive a free house. We would not have known that Hannah was handing out this word so frequently because she would have been on a different team each time.

Consistent teams and real-time coaching by team captains proved to be another advantage for improving the strength and integrity of our prophetic company.

With a very clear point person, growth, critique, and advanced learning could occur in the moment it was most needed—immediately following the appointment. The coach was able to pull Hannah aside and identify with her that perhaps she was ministering out of her own desire for a house. Hannah learned to not prophesy from her own needs and desires and was able to continue to serve on a prophetic team with real-time accountability. In the end, we came to understand that you can't grow from what you don't know.

Real-time coaching also helps with the type of person I will call Dark Dennis. Dennis is the guy who shares about the hard times you have been through and the dark, dark, dark tunnel ahead. Knowing our protocol, Dark Dennis will usually throw in a gratuitous, "But there is a light ahead" at the end of his depressing "prophecy." A real-time coach can identify prophetic tendencies that may need some deeper pastoring. They also afford the opportunity to speak to something right after it happens. For instance, if Dark Dennis gives his depressing word, we can gently cut in with more uplifting prophetic encouragement for the receiver and then speak an appropriate course correction to Dennis when the receiver has stepped away. We can also pastor Dennis about his fascination with dark "prophetic" words.

Coaches give us another level of true accountability in which we are not only being responsible for the words we speak, but accountable for how we deliver them, the motives behind our delivery, and our overall health as a team member. Because coaches are chosen for their people skills as well as prophetic grace, they can catch these little foxes before they spoil the whole vine.

Prophetic Synergy

I think another huge benefit of forming consistent teams is the possibility of achieving prophetic synergy. "Synergy" can be defined as "the interaction or cooperation of two or more agents to produce a combined effect greater than the sum of their separate effects."[29] Simply put, synergy in this context is the sense of chemistry that comes most often from spending time together. I've seen this happen so many times where we discover more of God's grace and wisdom through observing how others prophesy. By working together repeatedly, we can begin to anticipate when a fellow teammate has a sure word, is wrestling with a word, or simply needs some encouragement to speak out. By recognizing these signals in one another, we can call out greatness that so often waits for an invitation.

Throughout time, great leaders have recognized the value of structures that facilitate synergy. Aristotle said:

The whole is greater than the sum of its parts.

Isaiah the prophet said:

As the new wine is found in the cluster . . . do not destroy it, for a blessing is in it.

65:8, NKJV

Paul wrote how each of our gifts are like parts of a greater body.[30] More than getting the job done as prophetic teams, we desire to grow together, to partner for a greater third-heaven breakthrough, and to

---

[29] Google "Knowledge Graph".
[30] 1 Cor. 12.

grow in love for one another as we access greater measures of God's power and grace.

Team Members: The Encouragers

Each branch of our prophetic community contributes something specific and unique to the greater whole. We speak of our prophetic branches as spokes rather than levels because the different designations do not represent superior measures of prophetic prowess, but rather, the uniqueness of each contribution to the prophetic company where each member is valued and vital. Team members build the most fundamental and foundational element of prophetic community.

If Apostle Paul was correct when he said the one who prophesies is greater because he edifies the church and if Jesus said greatness is found in service, then our prophetic team members manifest a high level of greatness through their prophetic encouragement and service. We believe encouragement is the mother tongue of the Holy Spirit. Encouragement pours supernatural courage into people's lives to take ahold of earth-shaking destinies. Understanding this true nature of encouragement, the contribution of team members cannot be overstated or overlooked.

Coaches: The Pillars and Gatekeepers

Coaches, as mentioned before, are the gatekeepers of our prophetic protocol. Scripture tells us to judge and to test a word for we know in part and prophesy in part. Coaches make sure that our methods and our motives stay true to the Scripture and the character and nature of God. They keep our culture healthy through enforcing a real, measurable, and practical accountability.

The basic responsibilities of a coach in our community are as follows:

- They recruit their own team members subject to leadership approval.

- They pastor, encourage, and facilitate community within this team.

- They serve as the lead person in their prophetic group during team ministry.

- They reinforce our prophetic protocol.

- They perform real-time coaching, encouraging, and correcting of team members.

- They help with prophetic activations at our school of prophecy.

- They recommend team members whom they feel are qualified to become coaches.

- They attend a once-a-month coaches' meeting.

Coaches are connectors—pillars of true prophetic community. They manifest pastoral love and prophetic grace that create a sense of family where each part of the community can know and feel their connection to the whole. With a value for loving one another and building community, we follow the way of love while earnestly desiring spiritual gifts. Prophecy without love is noise. Coaches help us honor our goal of expressing our faith through love.

I'm so thankful for those who have partnered with us to build prophetic community. It's so much fun to work and discover together what is possible for a community of love and faith. I feel that we are just beginning to explore the benefits of functioning as a true prophetic company.

In the next chapter I will share the contribution and role of those I refer to as seers and mystics.

6

Seers and Mystics

One night as I prepared for bed, I felt the Lord saying, *Get up, and take your son to a movie.* I love movies, but the impression surprised me for several reasons. First of all, it was a school night, and it was already late. I didn't even know if any movies would still be showing. It also seemed like a strange thing for the Lord to say. I crept into my son's room. I think he was eleven years old at the time. Gently shaking him awake I whispered, "Michael, do you want to go to a movie?" He looked at me with an incredulous expression, wiped the sleep from his eyes, and said, "Sure."

By the time we were both dressed it was nearly eleven o'clock. Arriving at our local theater, I found that the only movie still showing was a Kung-Fu flick called *Crouching Tiger, Hidden Dragon*. The movie wasn't even in English; we had to read subtitles. All through the film, God poured out revelation on me. I was overwhelmed with the sense that He was giving me keys on how to mentor a double-portion generation.

At the end of the film, I was pretty undone. I knew why I had been sent there; but still, I felt the need to somehow redeem this movie or contextualize it for my son. So, after the movie we went to a little diner and sat down for a conversation and a coke.

During the film, there were all kinds of special effects with people flying through the air while performing amazing feats of combat. I started thinking that maybe I could use these visuals to share the realities of the spiritual world. So I made my first attempt at redeeming the movie for him by saying, "Michael, all of that flying around is just Hollywood, but the spirit world it represents is very real."

Sipping his coke, my boy casually answered back, "Oh, I know, Dad."

His answer somehow surprised me, so I asked, "What do you mean, you know?"

"Well," he explained, "I see things."

"What?" I asked. "What do you mean you 'see things'? What kind of things do you see?"

He took another sip of his soda and answered, "Oh, angels and demons and stuff."

"What?!" I was shocked. This was the first I had heard of it, so I thought I might test the accuracy of his claim.

"What do you mean? What do they look like?"

Michael answered nonchalantly, "It depends on what kind they are."

Okay, now I was kind of freaked out. How could he know about kinds of spirits? So I asked again, "What do you mean?"

"Well," he explained, "an afflicting spirit looks like a little three-foot monkey or imp with these four-inch claws that dig in from the outside. An unclean spirit looks like a really mean homeless person with red eyes. Warrior spirits are really big and carry weapons."

I think he might have continued if I hadn't stopped him with another question. "Wait a minute . . . how do you know all of this?" Last time I checked we didn't teach the rank-and-file of demonic authorities in Sunday school.

Michael answered, "I just see things, and I ask God what they are."

Seers

This late night encounter broadened my world once again. I have personally had some strange spiritual experiences where I saw or perceived things, but what my son referred to that night sounded more like a constant and often involuntary perception of the spirit realm. Once again, I poured into the record of Scripture, contemporary Christian writings, and revival history. The result was clear—seeing is a real operation of biblical spiritual gifts.

The first Scripture I looked at came from 2 Kings 6. Elisha and his servant Gehazi had been surrounded in the night by a hostile enemy army. When the servant stepped outside the next morning, he panicked at the sight of an army with horses and chariots that had surrounded the city. He ran to report his findings to the prophet. Elisha just prayed, "Open his eyes, Lord, so that he may see." Then the Lord opened the servant's eyes, and he saw the surrounding hills filled with celestial horses and chariots of fire encircling them. From this passage I understood that seeing angels or demons with the physical eyes must be a real thing.

Prophets and Seers

The Bible also revealed that prophets were once referred to as seers.[31] Yet, other places in Scripture they were differentiated as either a "prophet" or a "seer." The Hebrew assigned different words to each of these persons. *Chozeh* is the Hebrew word meaning "seer; a beholder in a vision; a stargazer." The word comes from an ancient root meaning "to see as a seer in the ecstatic state; to see, perceive with the intelligence or by experience."

Conversely, the word "prophet" used when the two appear together is most often the Hebrew word *nabiy. Nabiy* is formed from a root meaning "to speak, sing, or prophesy by inspiration, in prediction or discourse, under the influence of a divine spirit."

---

[31] 1 Sam. 9:9.

We can see from just a simple biblical word study that though the terms "prophet" and "seer" can be used interchangeably, there are sometimes also biblical distinctions between prophets and seers.

Mystics

Though "mystic" is not commonly a word used in Christian circles today, the *Oxford English Dictionary* defines it as "a person who tries to communicate directly with God; someone who attempts to be united with God through prayer." Currently, the word more often refers to "a person who achieves mystical experiences" or "one who practices mysticism." I believe this word can be helpful to describe people whose communion with God results in mysterious experiences or manifestations. Not only are there seers in this world, there are feelers, and hearers, and all sorts of mysterious operations of perceiving spiritual realms.

These perceptions are not demonic or evil; they stem from specific operations of spiritual gifts from a good God. I think the strength of using this term today is that it welcomes pre-Christians into a dialogue that produces real and redemptive answers, and it provides a clear category for people who are having extraordinary experiences with God without the fear of being vilified.

To persecute, vilify, or refute someone's spiritual impressions because we don't personally have the same practice or because we don't understand what is going on is to turn us back to the dark ages of ignorant Cessationism. The Spirit world is very real, and the Bible is full of varied interactions with this mysterious realm. Leaders would do better to ask more questions and make less judgments that we might learn how to come alongside of those who are having what could be called mystical experiences in God.

Seers and Mystics

Some assume that since seer and prophet were sometimes

synonymous in Scripture, that every seer is also a prophet. I disagree with that assumption. The operation of a manifestation gift is not an initiation into a ministry gift or office. The church often makes the mistake of prematurely exalting or persecuting the most gifted person in their midst. I know many seers who don't have good people skills or communication skills. Those deficiencies can make them dangerous if given too much position, authority, or opportunity based on the strength of their prophetic gift alone. Still, seers and mystics are vital to the health of any prophetic community.

One of the things I learned from the Holy Spirit through watching *Crouching Tiger, Hidden Dragon* is that I can still mentor people with greater gifts than my own. Oftentimes, believers share their mystical encounters with me, and God gives me an interpretation, understanding, or a word of wisdom that helps give a greater practicality to what otherwise would just seem strange. I believe imparting wisdom and a biblical context is a part of being ready to mentor a double-portion generation. Realize that the one with the gift does not always have the wisdom and maturity to process or be productive with his gifts. I have helped many tormented mystics bring their impressions into scriptural subjection and a place of healthy operation.

Wayne's World

Many years ago, I met a heavy-machine operator named Wayne. Wayne had a sixth-grade education and the emotional scars from two failed marriages. What many of us didn't realize was that Wayne had amazing spiritual gifts.

One day after teaching on spiritual gifts, Wayne approached me and said that he often would see or feel things that meant something. A few years earlier, he tried to talk with the pastor of his church about it, and he was told to suppress the feelings and not talk about them again. Wayne had agreed and stuffed his gifts for years.

I asked Wayne to describe some of the impressions, and he shared a story.

One day, he was eating in a restaurant and received really bad service from the waitress. Instead of getting angry, Wayne looked deep into her eyes and announced, "I know why you are so upset today."

The woman stopped and stared at Wayne. He continued, "Two years ago you had an abortion. You didn't want to do it, but you were pressured into it. You loved that baby, and you even named him Timothy. Taking a life is a serious thing, but God has forgiven you, and He loves you." The woman melted into a puddle of grace and forgiveness and was radically born again.

This was just a small sample of the gift that Wayne was told by his pastor to suppress.

At another time, Wayne met a man while evangelizing on the streets of San Francisco. He went over and sat on a park bench near the nervous gangbanger. Wayne said to him, "God told me you have a gun."

The man looked shocked and then flashed his pistol at Wayne. "God said you are about to do something that is going to ruin your life. You want to avenge the death of your brother, but that won't satisfy the emptiness you feel inside," Wayne continued. The gangbanger also melted into a puddle, repented of his intentions, and gave his life to Christ.

I asked Wayne to join my traveling ministry team, and we saw hundreds of miraculous healings, signs, and wonders by being a part of Wayne's world.

How much are we missing by discounting the prophetic impressions of seers and mystics?

Contributions to the Community

Our community started a once-a-month home group for seers and mystics like Wayne and my son. Anyone who was having unexplainable experiences was welcome to come and share their impressions with the group. The meeting provides a safe place to process, pray, and connect with others who have similar encounters. It's a place where people can build community with others who are having similar impressions and to gain growth and biblical context for the experiences they are having. From this place of a healthy and sound community, mystics and seers begin to make a significant contribution to the Body.

The primary contribution of seers within the prophetic community is in the area of consulting. I learned that often times I could perceive that something was going on but I didn't always know what it was. I love to consult with the seers and mystics to get a better consensus on what the Lord is doing.

Eyes on a Silver Platter

One example is from a Sunday morning service where I felt a strong healing presence of the Holy Spirit. I find it helpful when going after healing to be as specific as possible. This particular week, I just wasn't sure what to go after. I called over one of our seers during the worship. "Do you see anything?" I asked. He replied that he saw a big angel with a silver platter full of eyeballs. Now even though that is a very strange thing to see and communicate, I felt a very clear witness in my spirit. Without making reference to the angel, the platter, or the eyeballs, I announced that we would be praying for eye miracles. Many people came forward, and there were several great testimonies of healing. The week following this service, one of our staff members went in for an optical examine because her glasses had become really blurry. After the examination, the doctor said that the problem was that her eyes had improved so much, her prescription was too strong. Her healing came as a result of God's goodness and the consultation that came through a willing seer.

Handcuffs and a Mask

My now adult son also consults with me on occasion. I remember a healing line I was doing in a small town in Northern California many years ago. The first two people I prayed for had instant results and were completely healed. The ministry to the third person appeared to have no effect or significant change. I turned and asked my young son, "Do you see anything?"

He responded, "Yes. I see handcuffs on the person's wrists."

"Well, what should I do?" I asked.

He looked at me as if the answer was obvious and said, "Well, break them."

Honestly, I had no idea how to respond to that. I asked the person to close her eyes and lift her hands out in front of her. As a sheer act of faith and prophetic intercession, I made a chopping motion between her hands. Looking back at my son, he confirmed that the handcuffs were now broken.

I asked the person how she was doing, and to my surprise she happily responded, "I am completely healed!"

Further down the same prayer line, I again seemed to be getting no breakthrough. Again, I consulted with my son.

"That person has a hood on their head . . . like an executioner's mask," Michael informed me.

When I again inquired what should be done, he promptly answered, "Well . . . pull it off!"

Once again, I asked the receiver to close his eyes. I reached over his head with authority and faith and forcefully ripped off the invisible mask.

Michael nodded . . . the mask was gone, and once again, the recipient of the strange prophetic act reported a total healing.

What I began to learn from these experiences is that there is so much we miss when we limit our partnership with Holy Spirit to only what we know and understand. This is why God has made His church a body. This is where prophetic synergy comes from—valuing our differences. We make a place in our community for things we don't always understand. We value and dignify those who are having these encounters. It is the job of prophetic community to love and listen first and to ask questions later. There are differing gifts and differing operations. We need to embrace and encourage the variety of ways God moves among His people.

In the next chapter, we will discuss the role and contribution of prophets within our community.

7

Prophets

More than a decade ago, Kris Vallotton asked me if I would help him start the Bethel School of the Prophets. I was really honored at the invitation, but I felt inwardly pressed to challenge him, "Kris, I would love to teach at your school, but I don't think I'm a prophet."

Kris answered, "Don't you call out worship leaders who become the forefront of movements in nations?" I pondered this thought for a moment. "Well . . . yes," I admitted, "I guess so."

Kris replied with something very Kris-like, "Well, that's a prophet, so just shut up and do it."

My Journey to the Office

To be really honest with you, for many years, I thought that Kris just loved me and was including me in the grace of his own strong anointing. I taught in the school for several years, still wondering internally if I truly possessed the call of an office prophet. Then one year at the Bethel School of the Prophets in Redding, California, we invited James Goll, a well-known prophet and author of many books on the subject, to participate as a guest speaker. In the very first session of the school, James called me out, "Dano, stand up. The Lord says, 'You are a prophet after the order of Asaph to raise up the Levitical priesthood in worship and restore the tabernacle of David around the world . . .'" With many other words he encouraged me in my office call as a prophet.

Looking back on it, I don't know why I didn't believe Kris but did choose to believe James. I guess that I truly thought Kris was influenced by his love for me as a friend. I also think there were other factors affecting my hesitation to embrace this role. Somewhere deep inside, I must have believed that being a prophet would feel more other-worldly—more celestial. Giving prophecies and calling out leaders just felt natural to me, not like some special call to a prophetic office. Perhaps my reasoning testified to another form of Exceptionism? Yet, a very real part of my journey was my difficulty in accepting the fact that prophets are normal people like you and me, called by God to release grace over saints to hear, see, and know the heart and mind of God. While I count it a great honor, to this day I still don't feel like I'm something special or out-of-the-ordinary in my prophetic role.

Despite my early hesitations, I no longer question my call to that role in any way even though accepting that call has not felt any different to how I have always lived my life with the Lord.

Perhaps you, too, have felt the weight of wonder surrounding similar questions on what truly qualifies one as a prophet.

What Makes an Office Prophet?

How do we know who is called to be a prophet? Early on in the School of the Prophets, I learned an important criteria from a biblical narrative that we used for recognizing the office of prophet. Kris taught a biblical pattern based on the life of King David. David had three encounters before he entered his God-appointed office as king. The order of this biblical pattern doesn't matter.

- A personal call or inner conviction about the office.

• An outward confirmation from an apostle or prophet.

• A season of being received in the office by the people.

Young David received the outward call fourteen years before sitting for the first time in the official office of king.[32] After being called out by the prophet Samuel, David had an inner witness of the Spirit, and he began to take the new anointing for a test drive. He defeated Goliath, built an army in a desert, defended national borders, and interacted with other kings and rulers. Basically, David did everything a king could do even before he sat on the throne. By the time he was actually in the office of king, it was obvious to everyone that he belonged there.

The Patience of Elisha

The same might be said for Elisha's process. Elijah appointed Elisha as the newest prophet of Israel by the assignment of the Lord. He cast his own mantle on Elisha as a prophetic symbol of the transfer of authority.[33] Yet, Elisha did not enter that office right away. He chose to serve Elijah for many years. Though he had the anointing and calling of a prophet, Elisha found contentment in being known as the man who "used to pour water on the hands of Elijah."[34] I believe that Elisha's patience with the process and his servant heart are some of the qualities that qualified him later to be a double-portion prophet.

Notice how in both Elisha's and David's lives, the office came many years after the public anointing and the inner witness. If you have the call and anointing to be a prophet, don't rush to be recognized in the office. Just "do the stuff," and wait for the Lord to exalt you in the eyes of the people you are called to serve. Until you are received in the office by the people, you are not yet a prophet in the same way that David had not yet been enthroned as king. David didn't need a throne to behave like a king, and you don't need a prophetic office to live powerfully with your prophetic grace and gift. Be patient, and

---

[32] 1 Sam. 16:13.

[33] 1 Kings 19:19.

[34] 2 Kings 3:11.

wait upon the Lord, trusting that the gift He has given you will make itself evident in the fullness of time.

> *A man's gift makes room for him, and brings him before great men.*
>
> Proverbs 18:16, NKJV

> *Do you see someone skilled in their work? They will serve before kings; they will not serve before officials of low rank.*
>
> Proverbs 22:29

Multiple Prophets

Historically, a prophetic company was most often characterized by multiple prophets in a single place. You don't see this very often today. Even when a church or business recognizes the office of a prophet, there is usually only one in the house. In our house at The Mission, we are blessed with multiple people in the call and office of prophet. Though not every church will have even one local prophet, much less a company of prophets, I believe there is a New Testament precedent for multiple prophets in a single location.

> *[The church is . . .] built on the foundation of the apostles and prophets, with Christ Jesus himself as the chief cornerstone.*
>
> Ephesians 2:20

Notice in the above Scripture that the reference to apostles and prophets is plural. Not only do I believe that within a prophetic company, everyone can prophesy, I also believe a prophetic company makes room for multiple people in the office of prophet. The New Testament church certainly had multiple prophets in their community.

Spheres of Influence

One of the concepts that makes room for multiple prophets in a single location is the understanding of spheres of influence. This is another concept I learned in the School of the Prophets with Kris Vallotton. The basic idea is that your gift works everywhere on everyone but works best somewhere on someone. Paul spoke in his second epistle to the Corinthians about his own sphere of influence.

> *We, however, will not boast beyond proper limits, but will confine our boasting to the sphere of service God himself has assigned to us, a sphere that also includes you. We are not going too far in our boasting, as would be the case if we had not come to you, for we did get as far as you with the gospel of Christ. Neither do we go beyond our limits by boasting of work done by others. Our hope is that, as your faith continues to grow, our sphere of activity among you will greatly expand.*

2 Corinthians 10:13-15

In another place Paul stated:

> *Even though I may not be an apostle to others, surely I am to you! For you are the seal of my apostleship in the Lord.*

1 Corinthians 9:2

A prophet is not a prophet to everyone in every place; he or she is a prophet to someone in some place. My personal research on this subject would suggest that spheres of influence could be divided into three categories:

- geographic—a place,

- demographic—a person or people group, and

- sociographic—an interest.

You could also say that every prophet has a where, a who, and a what. The differences in our spheres of influence are what give us room to be a prophetic company. Prophets are not vying for the top position or "senior prophet" title in the church. Healthy communities of prophets recognize differing spheres of assignment and influence. Valuing these differences creates room for everyone to work and serve in a healthy culture of honor.

Types of Prophets

Another idea that creates room for multiple prophets in one location is the understanding that there are different types of prophets. Though the following concept is certainly an over-simplification and generalization of a really huge subject, I believe that personality types also affect the role, function, and assignments of prophets. Records of personality profiling began appearing on the scene as early as the fifth century BCE with Empedocles' distinctions of persons relating to the elements of air, earth, fire, and water. In the fourth century BCE, Hippocrates distinguished personalities through body fluids: blood, black bile, yellow bile, and phlegm. Plato, in the same century, took a more poetic approach by distinguishing four personality types as artistic, sensible, intuitive, and reasoning. The most popular, enduring, and widely used quartet of personality profiles came in the second century AD from Galen's distinctions of sanguine, melancholic, choleric, and phlegmatic.

There have been countless variations of these four personality types through the centuries, but the majority of all profiles appear in sets of four. I began to wonder if this trend hearkened back to the sixth century BCE with the vision of Ezekiel and the four living creatures.[35] Ezekiel observed a heavenly vision of four living creatures with the faces of a lion, a man, an ox, and an eagle. Borrowing these heavenly designations for a metaphorical moment might give us a better picture of the variety of prophetic roles and types revealed in Scripture.

A lion prophet would be the ruler, messenger, builder. Like the lion who is often culturally referred to as "king of the jungle," the lion-type prophet will often have a governmental or leadership role. This category would include biblical prophets like David, Deborah, Haggai, Samuel, and several New Testament prophets. Their main assignments would be to govern by word or deed and to build or create what God prophetically revealed.

The man-faced prophet could be distinguished as the counselor, strategist, ambassador. The man-face is significant because this prophet's assignment is often to serve a specific person. Daniel wasn't a ruler or builder (lion-type), but he served generations of leaders with his prophetic counsel, insights, and strategies. Abiathar consulted for King Saul. Gad was known as David's seer. Heman trained the worshiper seers that served in David's tabernacle. All of these biblical prophets could be considered man-faced prophets. This prophetic role most often comes alongside of strong leaders to advise, counsel, and strategize. The primary focus is not delivering a prophetic message but rather asking great prophetic questions, interpreting spiritual experiences, and giving wise prophetic counsel.

The ox-face of the heavenly creature represents prophets who are activists, agents, and miracle workers. Elijah and Elisha would both be in this category. Today we tend to think that prophets are almost exclusively "message prophets"—those who teach, preach, or are itinerant speakers or leaders. Yet, two of the greatest prophets in history wrote no books bearing their name and delivered very few prophetic messages. They represent the ox because they are the doers. The ox-face prophet does the work of a prophet without a lot of talk. This prophet *becomes* the message. Their ministry is often characterized

---

[35] Ezek. 1:5.

by miracles, signs, and wonders that are in themselves a prophetic statement. Not all office prophets have to be leaders or speakers.

The final face revealed in the pattern of the four living creatures is that of the eagle. An eagle prophet is the watchman, guardian, reformer. Visions and heavenly experiences define a strong characteristic of the eagle in the animal kingdom and the same is true for eagle prophets. Ezekiel certainly could be characterized as an eagle prophet. He lived in the spiritual high places and was given to extreme mystical spiritual encounters. Habakkuk could be classified as an eagle prophet; he stationed himself to watch and see what God would say. Jeremiah certainly served as a watchman and issued the cry of a reformer. These types of prophets are great writers and thinkers. Often an eagle prophet will be involved in prophetic intercession like the prophetic acts performed by Ezekiel and Hosea. This prophet by nature of his or her long-distance seeing will generally be more of a futurist.

Of course the danger in applying these types of classification lies with the tendency to limit people rather than using the information to identify and celebrate the validity of different expressions of the office of prophet. My goal is the latter. It is possible for a prophet to manifest different types of offices in various seasons. My purpose in the distinction is not to pigeon-hole anyone but to create room for multiple prophets by valuing the variety of operations and administration of the spiritual gifts and ministerial offices.

The Contributions of an Office Prophet

As I mentioned earlier, every spoke of our prophetic community makes multiple contributions to the whole. Our goal in these chapters is to recognize what are the defining or distinctive contributions of each spoke of our prophetic company. I believe one of the benefits of recognizing the office of prophet is the direction and prophetic counsel office prophets bring to the community. Prophets help us judge and discern the word of the Lord[36] and often assist in developing

---

[36] See 1 Cor. 14:29.

the strategies that help us pursue what God is saying.[37] Though I put value on the prophetic words of team members, coaches, and seers, it's probably fair to say that I place greater weight on a directional word that comes from a proven prophetic office. Make no mistake in what I am saying: anyone in the community can give a strong and accurate prophetic word. Prophets don't always represent the greatest level of gifting; however, because of the office, they have been called and entrusted by God with a different type of stewardship.

Developing Prophets

It is important that prophets be recognized by the people, but it is also important that others are contributing to the development of the prophet. Partnerships with apostles, teachers, and other fivefold leaders are essential to giving healthy feedback in judging and deciphering prophetic insights.

Another group that helps in the development of office prophets are our prophetic presbyters. I will define their role in the next chapter.

---

[37] See Acts 15:28.

8

Prophetic Presbytery

What is a presbytery? *Merriam Webster Dictionary* defines a presbytery as "a group of ministers and elders who are leaders of the church in a particular area." Paul referred to a spiritual presbytery in his writings to Timothy.

> *Neglect not the gift that is in thee, which was given thee by prophecy, with the laying on of the hands of the **presbytery**.*

> 1 Timothy 4:14, KJV, emphasis added

I used the *King James Version* here because it is one of the few versions that translates the Greek word *presbyterion* as "presbytery."

The laying on of hands by the presbytery that Paul is speaking of in this passage carries several biblical implications. First, the laying on of hands was considered an elementary teaching in the church by the writer of Hebrews.[38] Paul's narrative suggests that

---

[38] Heb. 6:1-2.

the laying on of hands includes impartation of spiritual gifts and graces.[39] Commissioning of assignments and leaders certainly formed a responsibility of the early prophetic presbytery.[40] Both Jesus and the post-resurrection disciples utilized the laying on of hands for the release of various spiritual blessings.[41] This First Timothy reference to a spiritual presbytery represents all of the fore-mentioned biblical uses for laying on of hands in one brief verse.

A presbytery can also be an event. Noted author and prophet Dr. Bill Hamon describes a prophetic presbytery as "an event where two or more prophets and/or prophetic ministers lay hands on and prophesy over individuals at a specified time and place."[42] Hamon cites several purposes for conducting a prophetic presbytery including revealing a church member's ministry in the Body of Christ, releasing a *rhema* word over individuals, imparting and activating divinely ordained gifts and graces, and commissioning five-fold leaders.

Prophetic Teams versus Prophetic Presbytery

Why do we need prophetic presbytery if we already have accurate, trained prophetic teams? Remember that the primary purpose of a prophetic team is to comfort, encourage, and build up. Within a prophetic ministry team appointment, it is possible to receive something that is instructional or directional, but the majority of input will be more of a blessing nature. That is because the primary purpose of the gift of prophecy is to release the ministry of encouragement.

Prophetic presbytery is a specific appointment with a different purpose and a different recognized level of authority. Though all prophecies must be judged—even those delivered by a prophet or prophetic presbytery—a prophetic presbytery would have more freedom and authority to speak words of counsel, direction, and

---

[39] Rom. 1:11.

[40] Acts 6:5-6; 13:2-4.

[41] Mark 8:23-25; Acts 9:17.

[42] Hamon, Dr. Bill. *Apostles, Prophets, and the Coming Moves of God.* Published by Destiny Image, 1997.

alignment. Presbytery appointments also involve more of the ministry of impartation and commissioning based upon the presbyters' recognized authority to do so as leaders in the faith community.

Our prophetic presbytery at The Mission is made up of prophets and church leaders with high-level prophetic giftings who are also known for their father/mother's heart. Presbytery members are recognized for their wisdom and counsel. Both heart and wisdom are essential for this position because we ask presbyters to be willing to walk through prophetic process with individuals. Rightly interpreting and applying a prophetic word is as important as correctly speaking one.

Consider the case of King Nebuchadnezzar. Nebuchadnezzar had a God-dream which Daniel interpreted, "You are that head of gold."[43] The inspiration was correct; the interpretation was correct; but the application was a disaster. Nebuchadnezzar built a ninety-foot tall golden statue of himself on the plains of Dura and required the world to bow down to it. This certainly is a huge misapplication of the prophetic interpretation stating that the king was the statue of gold.[44] Nebuchadnezzar's failure to rightly apply the prophetic word demonstrates the huge need for help in prophetic processing.

Prophetic presbytery helps us to walk out prophetic interpretations and applications with wisdom and counsel. In addition to the role of assisting in application of prophetic words, presbyters have permission, along with prophets and apostles, to call out five-fold gifts. We ask that prophetic team members and coaches not do so. Therefore, you can see that there is a value and a place for the role of both prophetic teams and prophetic presbytery.

Presbytery's Contribution to Community

Wise counsel is such an important contribution to the prophetic community. Our prophetic presbytery ministers almost exclusively to

---

[43] Dan. 2:38.

[44] Dan. 2-3.

church, world, and marketplace leaders. As I mentioned earlier, it's not that the presbytery's words are necessarily better or stronger than any other team member, but the delivery and content will be characterized by a greater maturity level of love, wisdom, and experience which makes them a more appropriate choice for ministering to those carrying a higher level of authority within the community. The main contribution of a presbyter to our prophetic community is in the prophetic processing piece I've already mentioned. Wise spiritual mothers and fathers help us not only rightly interpret prophetic words, but also come alongside in walking out the often challenging distance between process and promise.

Conclusion

The first distinctive of a prophetic community is that it is a place where everyone can prophesy. This doesn't mean that we all prophesy the same way or to the same level. That is why there are five contributing spokes to our prophetic community. The distinctions are a recognition of different roles, gift combinations, assignments, and manifestations of grace within the Body. A review of the five spokes that make up our prophetic company and their primary contributions to our prophetic community are listed below.

1. Team members release encouragement.

2. Team coaches help build community and ensure accountability.

3. Seers and mystics consult over mysteries and share prophetic insights.

4. Prophets give direction, prophetic wisdom, and help to formulate strategies.

5. Presbyters help mentor and monitor the health of the entire prophetic community and assist in prophetic process.

The following chapter will expound more on the how and the what of prophetic processing.

9

The Good Fight

Let's return to the primary question I'm confronting in this book, "What does a prophetic company look like?" In the last several chapters, we explored the idea that a prophetic company is a people who believe that everyone can prophesy—not just prophets but every son and daughter. This alone is a revolutionary concept in some circles, but we won't stop here in our definition of prophetic community.

Fighting with Prophetic Words

Another defining factor in the quality of prophetic community has to do with what the people do with prophetic words after they are received. In my Bible college, our instructors validated the use of prophecy today. However, they also taught that prophecy was only for confirmation and affirmation. I remember their answer concerning the question, "What should we do with our prophecies?' most often returned, "Put them on the back shelf and wait to see if they come true." The implication was that a true prophecy would come to pass by sovereignty alone and a false prophecy would not come true at all. Whether that is what they actually taught or not, I couldn't say, but that was certainly my perception of what was being taught and, more importantly, modeled in those days.

What Should We Do with Prophecies?

Living in the midst of vibrant prophetic company can cause quite a pile-up of prophetic words. By my thirties, I had my own stockpile of prophecies collecting dust on the back shelf while I waited for them to come true. Then a prophet named Byron Easterling and his wife Crystal volunteered to take our leadership team's primary prophetic words and process them for us. They spent a few months sorting through our personal prophetic words and extracting key themes and identities. When they finished, the Easterlings presented each of us with a packet that outlined who God says we are, the promises He had made to us, and an action plan detailing what we needed to do to align ourselves with the fulfillment of those promises and God's perception of who we are. I had never heard of something like this before, but I found the information and experience so incredibly helpful that our community began to pursue this on a larger scale. The prophet Graham Cooke was with us at the time, and he suggested we make a workshop out of our prophetic processing exercises. We called the workshop "The Good Fight" based upon Paul's instruction to his spiritual son Timothy.

> *This command I entrust to you, Timothy, my son, in accordance with the prophecies previously made concerning you, that by them you fight the good fight, keeping faith and a good conscience, which some have rejected and suffered shipwreck in regard to their faith.*

> 1 Timothy 1:18-19, NASB

Let's do a quick word study here to grasp a greater sense of the weight of these words. The phrase "fight the good fight" in the Greek is *strateuo kalos strateia*. The first word, *strateuo*, refers to going to war, battling, and being a soldier in active service. *Kalos*, translated as "good," is actually much stronger and broader in the Greek language. It means "beautiful, magnificent, excellent in nature and characteristics, honorable, noble, morally good." The final word, *strateia*, is the "expedition, campaign, or military service that you are enlisting in."

To put it all together we might say, "Take your prophetic words and engage in a noble campaign with them; approach it like a military operation; formulate a strategy." This idea is drastically different than the back-shelf approach that I had assumed in my earlier prophetic journey.

Jesus Goes to War

The Good Fight workshop was a huge success and proved to be a helpful tool for many people. This led me to research the concept even more. I dug into the New Testament and was struck with how Jesus fought with the words spoken over Him. In the following well-known passage, Jesus answered the devil's temptation with these words:

> *Man shall not live by bread alone, but by every word that proceeds from the mouth of God.*

> Matthew 4:4, NKJV

I understood that He was fighting the good fight with what had been spoken over Him. The devil challenged Jesus' identity as the Son of God by basically saying that if He truly *was* the Son, then He must prove it through turning stones to bread.

When Jesus spoke His famous response to the devil concerning the "word that proceeds from the mouth of God," He was not referencing the Bible. Though certainly the Bible is a standard for warfare and right living, Jesus fought the enemy with the word that had recently proceeded from the mouth of God. Remember that only days earlier at the baptism of Jesus, God the Father spoke from Heaven,

This is My Beloved Son, in whom I am well pleased.

Matthew 3:17, NKJV

As Satan tempted Jesus to prove by works what He already had by relationship, Jesus chose to remember and war with the word spoken over Him. He was, in essence, saying, "Devil, I don't have to prove anything to you. I just heard my Father speak from Heaven that I AM His Son and He is already pleased with Me!" Wow, that's a powerful declaration of war based upon what God the Father spoke over His Son.

Doers of the Word

This concept aligns well with the book of James' instruction to not merely listen to the word for that would be a deception; you must *do* what it says.[45] From my biblical research, I came to realize that what we were teaching concerning how to treat a prophetic word— just listen to the word and wait for it to come true—was wrong. We were unknowingly encouraging deception. When I speak of prophetic processing, I'm not talking about the error and foolishness of trying to self-fulfill prophecy. However, doing nothing with a prophecy is not only foolish, it is a deception. I think Paul's teaching in his first letter to the Thessalonians is helpful here.

> *Do not quench the Spirit. Do not treat prophecies with contempt but test them all; hold on to what is good, reject every kind of evil.*

1 Thessalonians 5:19-22

Not acting in partnership with our prophecies is a form of quenching the Holy Spirit and treating prophecy with contempt. The Greek

---

[45] James 1:22.

word for "contempt" literally means "to make no account of; to hold loosely; to lose esteem for; and to bring to naught, reduce to nothing." Searching other translations of this same passage, we find the word "test" interpreted as "examine," "scrutinize," and "judge." All of these biblical instructions command a very active approach to our prophetic words. I began to ask myself, *What am I doing to not treat prophetic words with contempt? How am I testing them, examining them, scrutinizing them? How would I hold on to them securely if I barely remembered what they said?* These became compelling questions for me in my own journey to define prophetic company, but this much became quite clear:

> **A prophetic company is a people who act on their prophetic words.**

Prophetic Processing

This new-found conviction that a prophetic company must be a people who war, fight with, and act on the noble causes of their prophetic words led me deeper into the exploration of how we should process our words. Since prophetic processing is not the primary focus of this book and because I am currently completing a book on the subject, I won't go into all the particulars of prophetic processing at this time. I will, however, give you the basics of how we learned to process prophetic words.

Sort, Judge, and Test the Prophecy

Our first step in prophetic processing is to sort, judge, and test the words. Obviously, we discard anything that is contrary to the written Word or the character and nature of God. We also take note of the source:

- Who spoke the word?

- What were the circumstances in which the word was delivered?

- How well does the word resonate with your own spirit?

The instruction in First Corinthians chapter fourteen is that two or three people should prophesy and the rest should judge.[46] This passage shows us that judging, examining, and testing prophecy should be done in the company of loved ones and leaders, not alone. Judging prophecy is a team sport.

Gather the "Now" Words

This practice of processing in the context of community protects us from errors of misinterpretation and addresses our potential blind spots. For our processing exercises, we ask students to choose the three personal prophecies they feel are the "now word" of the Lord for them—the ones they most resonate with in this season. It's difficult to process more than three-to-five words at a time. Next, we ask participants to bring those three words typed out, double-spaced, and printed on sheets of paper to make them easier to process.

Processing Prophetic Identity

With these strong personal words in hand, we next process prophetic identity. I believe that the two most important questions in the kingdom of God are, "Who do you say that Jesus is?" and "Who does Jesus say that you are?" What you say about Jesus is the key to getting you into Heaven; what Jesus says about you is a key to getting heaven into you. After all, the truest thing about you in the universe is what God says.

Many Christians are still externally or internally defined. We are defined by our circumstances, performance, the opinions of others, or by our opinions of ourselves. All of these sources are particularly subject to error. The goal is not to be externally or internally defined, but to be eternally defined: who does Heaven say that you are?

---

[46] 1 Cor. 14:29.

What if prophecy is simply overhearing how you are already known and seen in heavenly places in Christ Jesus? This might have been the case in the story of Gideon.

Gideon's Heavenly Identity

I find the story of Gideon's angelic encounter fascinating. An angel of the Lord appears to Gideon with the greeting,

> *The LORD is with you, mighty warrior.*

> Judges 6:12

Gideon was confused by the greeting because he didn't see himself in any way as a mighty warrior. He was at that very time hiding out in a winepress trying to tread out a little wheat for his family.

Gideon's internal and external definers were off the mark. He saw himself only as the weakest and the least.

> *"Pardon me, my lord," Gideon replied, "but how can I save Israel? My clan is the weakest in Manasseh, and I am the least in my family."*

> Judges 6:15

But what if Gideon was already known as a mighty warrior in Heaven? When the angel came down to address him, he was not mocking his weakness; he was revealing his heavenly identity. In the earthly realm, we would only call someone a mighty warrior who had already won battles and shown themselves valiant in warfare. In the heavenly kingdom, you win battles because God says you are a mighty warrior.

In the kingdom of God, identity comes first, Graham Cooke says, "You're a human being, not a human doing." This is why starting with who God says you are in prophetic words is so important. The Bible, God's written word, primarily speaks to our corporate identity as sons and daughters, but God's personal prophetic words to us speak to our individuality as sons and daughters and as new creations.

Calling Out Heavenly Identity in Prophetic Companies

Prophetic identity becomes an important component in prophetic companies because we make it our goal to know one another after our new creation rather than by our historical performance. Paul said it this way:

> *So from now on we regard no one from a worldly point of view. Though we once regarded Christ in this way, we do so no longer. Therefore, if anyone is in Christ, the new creation has come: The old is gone, the new is here!*

> 2 Corinthians 5:16-17

A revelation of heavenly identity through prophetic processing allows us to address one another in an entirely different way. Paul said that they used to regard Christ in an earthly way. From an earthly perspective, Jesus was Mary and Joseph's son, a carpenter, a good teacher, and a profound prophet. Yet, in Jesus' discourse with His disciples concerning His identity, none of these were a satisfactory description. It was the impetuous Peter who had the heavenly revelation of Jesus, "You are the Christ, the Son of the Living God."[47] Jesus replied that only the Father in Heaven could reveal that to him. Each one of us possesses a heavenly identity that only the Father can reveal. Your heavenly man is the truest you. In a prophetic company, when we begin to treat one another after our heavenly identity, drastic changes occur.

First of all, prophetic identity allows us to have a deeper honor and

---

[47] Matt. 16:13-20.

love for one another. Secondly, it changes the nature of accountability. Typically, accountability in the church has been holding someone to a standard slightly above the lowest common denominators. "Are you cheating on your taxes? Are you lying? Are you unfaithful to your spouse? Are you addicted to any substances?" If the answer to these questions is negative, "No, I'm not doing any of those things . . . ," then we assume that our friend is doing well as a believer. This is pathetic.

Accountability should not be calling each other out for our sins but calling each other *up* to our highest calling. With a revelation of our heavenly man, we are empowered to call one another to live at the standard of the revelation of their heavenly identity. Now, even if someone is misbehaving or under-performing, we call them up, "Hey, you are way too awesome to be acting like this. How does your current behavior align with who God says that you are?" Suddenly we are not attempting to live just above the acceptable line; we are setting our minds and hearts on things above and not on earthly things.[48]

The revelation of prophetic identity empowers us to live as healthier, happier, and holier people.

Processing the Language of Promise

After discovering who we are in Christ, we have a better context for analyzing what God says we will do. This comes in the form of prophetic promise. Both biblical and prophetic promises come in two forms: one is absolute and the other is conditional. Absolute promise is based upon God's declared intention toward us. This part of your prophetic word is as much a statement of fact as it is a promise. When God says that He will do something, He is completely faithful to His word.

At other times, God will issue conditional promises or promises that require some level of partnership. He might say something like, "As you seek My face, I will pour out a greater spirit of revelation

---

[48]   Col. 3:1-2.

and knowledge." This promise is conditional and requires an action on the part of the receiver to initiate what God is desiring to release. Prophetic promises must be processed to discern which promises are absolute and which ones require partnership.

Absolute promises still benefit from our agreement. As we declare and believe what God has absolutely promised to do, our faith and agreement can at times accelerate the outcome. In the case of conditional promise, the speed of our obedience always determines the rate of our acceleration. In some respects, you are currently moving at the speed of your own obedience. Conditional promises would never be fulfilled with the former back-shelf philosophy I possessed concerning how to treat prophecy. These promises must be moved to a front-shelf position and acted on for this promise to have any potential of life. You must enlist in a campaign with conditional promises.

I have a son whose primary love language is quality time, and he has little value for gifts. The funny thing is you can give this son gifts, money, and gift cards, and those gifts will just sit in their original packaging for months or even years. My wife and I have been frustrated many times to find an expired gift card in the dark recesses of his room. But isn't that what a lot of our prophecies are like? How many uncashed prophetic checks do you have sitting around—promises of God that you just never took to the bank? Processing prophetic promise helps us to form a MAP, that is, a Ministry Action Plan that aligns and appropriates our actions with the conditional promises God has spoken over us.

Processing Types and Metaphors

Another area of processing takes on the form of interpreting types and metaphors. For instance, when God says through a prophetic word that you are like an oak tree, that is a very different message from Him saying you are like an evergreen tree. The type of tree and the qualities of that tree are an important qualifier to what the message is saying. Prophetic revelation needs to be rooted in knowledge and understanding. This is true because Scripture teaches that we know in part and prophesy in part.[49] Prophecies and revelations arrive in partial form. Whenever we treat a part like a whole, we are subject to deception.

We encourage believers to study the types and metaphors given in their prophetic words to develop a clearer understanding of what God might be saying. For instance, I've met many students in our school of supernatural ministry who have received a word stating they have a Heidi Baker anointing. Heidi Baker is an amazing revivalist who feeds thousands of children every day in Africa. But that prophecy doesn't tell how they are like Heidi Baker. Does it mean they should move to Africa? Start a children's ministry? Feed the hungry? Fall on the floor and sing in the Spirit as Heidi is known to do? Further revelation is needed on what the Father is saying through this typology. You may want to read a biography of someone who you are prophetically compared to or watch a documentary on a type of thing or animal you are compared too. God will give you additional insights as you study and create an understanding root system for the initial prophetic revelation.

Processing Times, Seasons, and Numbers

I'm convinced that God often uses a different clock and numbering system than we do. Although many prophecies in Scripture were accurately fulfilled to the very day and hour, other timing words seem to be more of a typology than a literal timetable. Understanding times and seasons is an important part of rightly processing a prophetic word.

While processing, we look for indicators that speak of timing. Immediate language like "now" can be applied to your present situations, but words like "soon" speak of a season yet coming. Other prophetic promises may contain far off language. Remember that Joseph's dream, David's call, and Abraham's promise were all speaking to fulfillments at least a decade away. Some prophetic promises span

---

[49] 1 Cor. 13:9.

hundreds of years. All that is to say that discerning times and seasons is important to how we interact with personal and corporate prophecy.

Numbers in Scripture can also have a literal or a figurative meaning. For instance, when Jesus said that we must forgive seventy-seven times, He wasn't speaking literally but metaphorically.[50] Yet, when Jesus said that as Jonah was three days and nights in the belly of a huge fish, so the Son of Man would be three days and nights in the heart of the earth, He was making a literal statement of numbers and time.[51] Because prophecy includes both literal and figurative times, we must carefully process what God is saying whenever numbers are used in a prophetic word.

"In Ten Days"

I remember a student in our school of supernatural ministry who was very frustrated. She had received a word that said, "In ten days your whole life is going to change." The word really resonated with this young lady, so she fasted and prayed and prepared herself for a life-changing encounter. The ten days came and went with no epiphany. Months later this young lady was at one of my meetings, and she was very frustrated and disillusioned with the concept of prophecy and prophetic processing.

As she shared her struggle with me, I was immediately reminded of the figurative nature of some prophetic words and the importance of rightly discerning times and seasons.

I asked her, "Did your prophetic word say, 'In the next ten days'?"

She looked at me quizzically and then answered, "No, I guess not." I informed her that if she felt like this was a real word from the Lord that came from a credible source, she should not give up on the word. God didn't promise He would change her life in the following ten days, but rather, that there would be a ten-day time period in her life that would totally rewrite her story. She left greatly encouraged.

---

[50] Matt. 18:21-22.
[51] Matt. 12:40.

Times and seasons can be mysterious. The prophet Habakkuk added to this mystery by stating this paradox:

> *For the revelation awaits an appointed time; it speaks*
> *of the end and will not prove false. Though it linger,*
> *wait for it; it will certainly come and will not delay.*

Habakkuk 2:3

This passage accurately describes my journey with prophetic timing, "Though it linger . . . it will not delay." I heard someone say once that God is never late but He misses a lot of great opportunities to be early. God's timing is perfect, but it often doesn't fit our expectation of when He should come. That is why processing prophecies in a team is so important.

Invest in the Processing

There is much more to our prophetic processing technique, but you can see from what I have shared here that processing prophetic words is another foundation of our prophetic company. Prophetic communities take the time to invest in rightly processing their personal and corporate prophetic words. We choose to view one another from a heavenly perspective rather than according to our earthly limitations. We fight together to see prophetic destiny fulfilled and accelerated.

In the next chapter I will share the final defining quality of our prophetic company.

10

Prophetic Diversity

What if there were only one color of flower? What if there were one flavor of food or drink? What if everyone looked similar? Creation reveals the nature of God as well as God's love and value for variety.[52] Though mankind also enjoys variety, there can be a tendency in religious circles to create one way for how things should be done or seen. We make everything one flavor.

Manifold Wisdom

Paul the Apostle reveals that this tendency misses God's intent for His church, which is to make known the manifold wisdom of God to rulers and authorities in heavenly realms.[53] The word "manifold" means "variegated, marked with a great variety of colors, much varied." Wisdom and grace are meant to be expressed and revealed by the church as multicolored with varied flavors.

Unity in the church is not achieved through sameness but rather

---

[52] Rom. 1:18-20.

[53] Eph. 3:10.

by embracing and honoring diversity. Even the word for "agree" in the Bible, *symphoneo*, means to be harmonious or sound together. This Greek word reminds us of our English word "symphony." Symphonies do not all play the same part or instrument; the beauty and harmonious nature of the music comes from each one playing his unique part. This is the picture God always creates of spiritual gifts and the Body of Christ. In an earlier chapter, I disclosed some of the different expressions of the gift of the office of prophet. In this chapter, I would like to explore the variations in the gift of prophecy in what I call the three-dimensional nature of spiritual gifts.

Three-Dimensional Nature

There is a curious Scripture in the book of First John that says we have no need of anyone to teach us because His anointing teaches us all things.[54] What is curious is that God is the one who appointed teachers to equip the saints for works of service. Of course, God values teachers. The context of this passage is speaking specifically about the anointing. We might say concerning this passage that when it comes to the anointing, no one but the Holy Spirit can teach you everything. The reason that no man could teach you everything about the anointing is because there are nearly limitless combinations and permutations of variances in spiritual gifts.

When Paul taught spiritual gifts to the Corinthian church, they had a background of believing different gifts and virtues came from different gods. The apostle revealed that all the gifts came from one and the same Spirit, but Paul clearly taught a variety in gifts and expressions. In the midst of his discourse, Paul describes these gifts in three dimensions. Let's look at the passage.

> *There are different kinds of gifts, but the same Spirit distributes them. There are different kinds of service, but the same Lord. There are different kinds of*

---

[54] 1 John 2:27.

working, but in all of them and in everyone it is the
same God at work.

1 Corinthians 12:4-6

I've drawn from this passage the concept of a three-dimensional nature to spiritual gifts.

The First Dimension

As you already know, I was brought up in a cessationist background which taught that the gifts are no longer for today. Later, as I discovered the reality of spiritual gifts, my experience and exposure was limited to the nine manifestation gifts of First Corinthians chapter twelve. Yet as I read through the Bible, I found other lists and minor mentions of additional gifts. These multiple locations used the same Greek word for "gift" as the passage in First Corinthians. As I researched the work of theologians and scholars, I found that many people divided the gifts into various categories.

Some might categorize First Corinthians 12 as the manifestation gifts based upon the following verse.

Now to each one the manifestation of the Spirit is
given for the common good.

v. 7

Romans chapter twelve lists seven different gifts: prophesying, serving, teaching, encouraging, giving, leading, and showing mercy.[55] Bill Gothard of the Institute in Basic Life Principles categorizes these as the motivational gifts.

There is also the category of the five-fold ministerial gifts listed in Ephesians 4:11. I have referenced this list several times already in this book.

---

[55] Rom. 12:6-8.

I share these different types of gifts because, in my spiritual journey, I had to move from a place of not knowing or believing in gifts to embracing the fact that there are many different colors, flavors, and expressions of gifts working throughout the Body of Christ. This variety of spiritual gifts referred to in 1 Corinthians 12:4 forms the basic understanding of gifts in the first dimension.

The Second Dimension

The second dimension of spiritual gifts is that each of these gifts will have varying services, assignments, or administrations. The same gift will function differently within different settings or contexts. For instance, while researching several great historical revivalists, I found that many different gifts could display themselves in a service of healing. Smith Wigglesworth was known as a great faith healer, but more accurately we could say that Smith possessed a gift of faith with an assignment and passion for healing. The gift of faith (first dimension) worked in a service of healing (second dimension).

William Branham used words of knowledge (first dimension) to release a service or administration of healing (second dimension). He would also reference the presence of angels who were assisting in the work of healing by accessing a gift of discerning of spirits. So we might say that Branham operated in the gifts of words of knowledge and discerning of spirits with a service of healing.

Maria Woodworth Etter manifested a five-fold call to the gift of an evangelist. In Maria's writings, she shared her fear that if she started flowing in her great healing gift that it would draw only Christians and she might lose the opportunity to evangelize the lost. You might say that Maria had a gift of healing (first dimension) with a service of evangelism (second dimension).

By the time we get to the second dimension, we can already see that the possibilities for combinations of gifts and services are nearly endless. That is why the Holy Spirit has such a unique role in teaching us about our anointing.

The Third Dimension

Different workings and operations distinguish the third dimension. Teaching prophetic schools for more than two decades, I have encountered a wide variety of workings and operations of the gift of prophecy. Some people hear the information, some people see it, others feel it, and then there are those who just know. But even in each of these realms, there are variations of operations and workings. Seers can see in various ways. Some see the spirit realm with their natural eyes, some see in their imagination, while some see spiritual information in what is naturally perceived. All of these expressions of seeing have a biblical root that reveals the truth that there is not only one way of seeing. But seeing is not listed as a gift of the spirit; seeing is an operation or working of several of the gifts of the spirit.

Other senses can be used to operate or work in gifts of the Spirit. I've met people who smelled or tasted the presence of angels or demons. Years ago, on a trip to England where we held a huge tent crusade, one of the team members slipped away to hitchhike around the country. We slaved away in our crusade tent night and day for a week battling stale atmospheres, unseasonable weather, and limited attendance with very disappointing results. The hitchhiker arrived back at the airport to report the conversions of over 21 people. When I asked about his evangelism method, he told me that he would hold someone's hand while he prayed. Then he would have the person smell his hand, and the recipient would experience some distinct past memory revealed through olfaction or the sense of smell. The recollection would be so dramatic that he could then share the love of God, and the person would be saved. I had never heard of such a thing before. Before you pass judgment on this strange hitchhiker as a heretic, know that the army-fatigue-clad young man held four doctoral degrees in theology. He displayed a gift of word of knowledge (first dimension knowledge of past events), a gift of evangelism (second dimension service or administration), and an unusual operation or working through smell (third dimension).

Variety in Prophetic Company

While this story may seem like a particularly unusual application, it really shows the dimensionality of our spiritual gifts. No wonder Scripture says that when it comes to your anointing, no man can teach you, but the Holy Spirit will teach you all things.

As I began to understand the dimensionality of spiritual gifts, it revealed our final foundation for the formation of prophetic company.

A prophetic company is a people who value prophetic diversity.

In the same way that we discovered there is more than one type of prophet, we can see that there is more than one flavor or color of prophetic gift. As a matter of fact, the prophetic is itself a revelation of the manifold wisdom of God. A prophetic community must have a value system for prophetic diversity.

One of the places this diversity first manifested in our community was the call to view prophecy as a life skill not just a ministry skill. Kris Vallotton talks about how training in the zoo for life in the jungle is not helpful because these environments have different realities. I think a lot of churches train in prophetic ministry and then take the exact same form or model out into the streets. For instance, in church we tend to get into small groups and put one person in the center to receive encouraging prophetic words from the others. When churches think of prophetic ministry out in the world, they tend to take the exact same expression to the streets. They put up a sign that says "ENCOURAGING WORDS" or "DISCOVER YOUR FUTURE." Brave or curious onlookers come by and are surrounded by two or three team members who then perform typical prophetic ministry over them. This is a great method, and I am in no way criticizing this practice. I'm only saying that there are many more effective ways prophetic ministry can be taken outside the church.

Mom's Prophetic Sense

Consider prophecy within the mountain of family. I remember a short season in my teen years when I started to run from the call of God. I spent some time at parties and with girls who didn't have the same values as those I was trying to uphold. The funny thing is that right when I was about to step over the edge into an unwise decision, my mom would show up or call on the phone. Now you must realize here that my mom would not consider herself prophetic, but she sure had a keen spiritual sense for knowing where I was and the exact right time to intervene. I'm convinced that this is an expression of prophetic diversity in the mountain of family.

The Prophetic—A Life Skill

Prophecy is meant to be a life skill, not just a ministry skill. We can access the value of personal prophetic insight in parenting, financial decisions, career challenges, and many other practical areas.

The prophetic, after all, is the discerning of God's voice, heart, and mind on any subject at any given time. God graciously gives the believer access to His thoughts through prophetic grace by the Spirit of Truth.[56] This accessibility to the genius of the universe on any given subject is one of the greatest treasures of the abundant life.

In the next chapter, I will share how we have trained our prophetic community to begin to access these treasures of wisdom and knowledge in various forms and dimensions.

---

[56] 1 Cor. 2:12-16.

11

Training Prophetic Company

Smith Wigglesworth definitely ranks as one of my favorite spiritual heroes. Smith is credited with thousands of healing miracles and the resurrection of no less that fourteen people, including his wife. One day, as I read some transcribed messages of Wigglesworth's, I came across his quote:

If God is not moving, I move God.

The first time I read it, I slammed the book closed and said, "That's heresy. We can't move God!"

Riding a Wave or Making a Wave

I remained agitated at the thought and the book for a few days. Slowly, the Lord started reminding me of several passages in Isaiah where God said He was appalled that no one stirred themselves to take hold of Him.[57] Second Chronicles 16:9 states that God's eyes range

---

[57] See Isa. 59:16, 63:5, 64:4-7.

throughout the whole earth looking for those whose hearts are fully committed to Him so that He can show Himself strong of their behalf. I began to see that God actually *is* looking for people who will "move Him."

As I continued my journey on the subject of "stirring" in the New Testament, I found Scriptures about "stirring ourselves up in spiritual gifts" and "spurring one another on toward love and good works."[58] I think I had assumed that a supernatural lifestyle could only legitimately be initiated by a sovereign source. My thought would have been, *If God's not moving, don't move.* In my previous view of God's sovereignty, I thought one could only speak in tongues or prophesy if they were feeling a strong unction of the Holy Spirit to do so. I also thought that one could only step out in healing under His divine prompting. This left the realm of the supernatural as a possibility but only in special circumstances where there was a strong leading of the Spirit of God to act.

Supernatural Sons, Not Slaves

My basic misunderstanding on how and when God moves was just another example of flawed Exceptionism and a misconception of the true nature of sonship. Slaves only obey their masters, but sons act on what has been modeled in their household. I had been living like a slave waiting to be commanded rather than like a son who understood the values and vision of a healthy, holy household.

Believers are called to be about their Father's business. The supernatural is not only a sovereign event; it is a divine partnership. I came to see the supernatural as God's "super" plus my "natural." Sometimes God would initiate a spiritual event, and I would respond in faith and obedience; other times, I would initiate an act of faith in line with the Word and will of God, and the Spirit would jump in and join me. Though I constantly seek what God is saying and doing, I am not a robot or slave who doesn't know the ways of the Lord.

---

[58] See 2 Tim. 1:6; Heb. 10:24.

Take it to the Spirit-Gym

As I continued to experiment with this new understanding of my freedom to move God, I definitely saw an increase in the number of miraculous encounters and divine appointments. I became confident that there was something significant to viewing the supernatural lifestyle as a divine partnership rather than only a sovereign event that required spiritual unction and prodding.

It was during this season of discovery that I came across the Greek word *gymnazo*. I was particularly drawn to two scriptural references that used this word.

> *Have nothing to do with godless myths and old wives'*
> *tales; rather, train yourself to be godly.*
>
> 1 Timothy 4:7

> *But solid food is for the mature, who by constant use*
> *have trained themselves to distinguish good from evil.*
>
> Hebrews 5:14

Both of these verses speak of training ourselves. As I looked up the word in the original language for better understanding, I found the word *gymnazo* means "to exercise vigorously in any way, either the body or the mind." Gymnazo is like our English word "gymnasium." It was through this word study and these Bible passages that I came to further realize that God was inviting me to take my spirituality to the gym and give it a workout. It only stands to reason then that the form and depth of my training should match my expectation of encounter. If I wanted to prophesy to presidents and kings, I needed to exercise my grace and my faith at that level.

What if church is supposed to be less like a lecture hall and more like a spiritual gymnasium where we come and workout the spiritual faith and muscle required to do the works of Him who sent us?

Spiritual Exercise

Our team began to take the concept of spiritual exercise seriously. Because of the foundation laid by great prophetic teachers, I felt like our community possessed a reasonably sound doctrinal understanding of prophecy but were still relatively weak in the actual advanced exercise of the gifts.

I wondered, *What if the next level of our prophetic training were more about doing and less about teaching?* After all, the book of Acts starts with a recounting of everything that Jesus "began to do and teach."[59] I noted that in the book of the Acts of the Apostles, the doing-portion came first. This seemed to be Jesus' method for training His disciples as well. After calling them, He immediately sent them out with power and authority to "drive out all demons and to cure diseases."[60]

To experiment with this training model, we started a prophetic activation school. Once a month on a Friday night from 7:30-10:00, our entire prophetic community would meet for activation in prophetic ministry. The program ratio was 70 percent activation and mobilization to 30 percent teaching and testimony. Our emphasis became training by doing.

Over the years, we developed a multi-year, multi-tiered activation school. The first year focuses on the different ways to hear or discern the voice of God and a variety of ways to deliver a prophetic message. While the default mode for prophesying remains to this day—do or say whatever Holy Spirit reveals—we also learned several ways to stir up the gifts of God that are within us. We teach our people how to prophesy through a name, a visual stimulus, and through their senses. We also teach people to use intentional acts, the giving of gifts, written messages, art, and music as prophetic avenues. We teach on words of knowledge and how to prophesy through them. We explore prophesying over friends, family, and strangers as well as over

---

[59] Acts 1:1.
[60] Luke 9:1.

cities, regions, and nations.[61] The school has proven really fun. People are learning prophecy by doing and truly advancing the depth and understanding of their spiritual gifts.

Intermediate Training

While our beginner focus starts with the variety of ways to hear God and deliver a prophetic word, our intermediate track is exploring the theme of prophecy as a life skill rather than just a ministry skill. Each month, we take one of the seven mountains of influence—family, education, government, business, media, arts and entertainment, religion—and focus on what prophecy might look like in that specific context.

In addition to the new life-skills focus of our subject matter, we also began to train dimensionally with spiritual time zones. Let me explain. Since the Lord is the One who was, and is, and is to come,[62] we practice discerning and receiving information from the past, present, and future. Each month we perform exercises in the word of knowledge by releasing words of fact from the past-to-present time zone.

For instance, if we are focusing on the mountain of education, we instruct the students to find a partner they don't know well and tell the partner three things about a school he or she went to. Students are to focus on receiving information from God—like the name of the school, the school colors or mascot, or a favorite subject or teacher—with no input from the partner. Each participant is to perceive three pieces of information from a fellow student's past that they could only know by the Spirit of God.

---

[61] All of this material is in my *Basic Training in Prophetic Activation* manual and is available in paperback and digital format from Amazon.com or MissionVacaville.org.

[62] Rev. 4:8.

Training by Repetition

In doing these activations, we also discovered the power of repetition. To better understand why repetition is important to our prophetic training, let's return to the passage in Hebrews that utilizes the Greek word *gymnazo*.

> But solid food is for the mature, who by **constant use**
> have trained themselves to distinguish good from evil.

5:14, emphasis added

"Constant use" is the Greek word *hexis* which means "a power acquired by custom, practice, use; a habit of the body or mind." Taking from what we already know of the word training, we might paraphrase this passage by saying, "Mature prophetic people train themselves by making a habit of exercising their gifts vigorously and practicing regularly with their perceptions." If training yourself is like going to a spiritual gym, then it only makes sense to do reps—repeat the exercises over and over. We made a habit in our activation schools of doing most exercises multiple times. Here is what we found.

In the aforementioned word-of-knowledge drill—discerning information from the past about someone's school—we repeat the exercise three times. In the first round, perhaps two or three out of 100 students would get every answer correct. After polling the success rates and celebrating all the results, we would say, "Now, because we believe in training by repetition, get a new partner and do the same exercise again." The crowd of trainees often groan a little at first but then move into their second round of action. In the second round, the number would rise to five or six with all three pieces of information correct. By the third round, ten to twenty people would get every answer correct. I will tell you later what we did for those who got none of their clues correct.

We repeat this pattern of training until everyone has done the word of knowledge activation at least three times on three different people.

An amazing pattern emerged. After practicing this type of word of knowledge drill just three times (about 15-20 minutes total time), the number of people who would get every answer correct would jump exponentially. In several instances as many as 40 percent of the crowd would get all three answers correct just by practicing three times in about fifteen minutes. Consistently, every person in the class would increase their accuracy with just a little repetition practice. With this kind of payoff, repetition became a regular part of our prophetic activation training.

Weight Repetition

The next form of training we use is what I like to call weight training. At the physical gym, you can't expect to increase your muscle mass by repetition only. Along with the repetition, you must keep putting more weight on the bar. In our prophetic application, putting more weight on the bar is equal to taking greater risks to increase our measure of faith. Romans chapter twelve reveals the truth that each of us prophesies "in proportion to the measure of our faith." I'm convinced that the measure is not necessarily the size of the faith itself—how much you have—since God has given each one a measure of faith.[63] The measure has to do with the size of your expectation—how much you are believing for. Measure is about the application of your faith. Taking a larger risk increases the size of our expectation and enlarges our faith.

Let's take the example of words of knowledge for healing. I've been in many churches where people practice giving words of knowledge to release the ministry of healing. Typically, a person stands before the people and begins to list impressions of pain, sickness, or disease. The minister might say something like, "Someone here has pain in the right shoulder" or "I feel like there is a person here with a heart condition." If there is someone present with this need, he or she responds by going forward for prayer. I have seen many people healed with this method of pairing word of knowledge gift with healing gifts.

---

[63] Rom. 12:3.

However, if you want to grow in the word of knowledge gift, you have to move beyond this introductory level. To advance to the intermediate level—to put more weight on the bar—we ask our prophetic students to press in for more information from Holy Spirit, e.g., is the injured person male or female? What color is he or she wearing? How did the injury occur? By pressing in for more information, the words get much more specific and require a greater level of risk and faith, which in turn increases the level of faith in the room.

After we become comfortable with one level of ministry through repetition, it is our responsibility in training ourselves to put more weight on the bar and to take a higher level of risk.

Resistance Repetition

The third training method we discovered is resistance training. Resistance training speaks of how we respond to rejection and perceived personal failure. When I walk into the gym, I can't usually lift my target weight the first time. I must start at a lesser weight and then through repetition and regular practice, I slowly increase the weight I put on the bar until I reach my target goal. This means that my growth must embrace the reality of failure. I told you earlier that we celebrate the results of our efforts to flow in word of knowledge. What I haven't told you yet is that we give the biggest round of applause to those who missed all three clues. We don't celebrate error or mistakes, but rather, we celebrate risk, faith, and obedience with a standing ovation!

Fear of a False Word

In order to have a healthy prophetic community, there must be an environment where it is safe to take risks. Most people are so afraid that a wrong or half-right word makes them a false prophet that they are fearful of stepping out to try anything. A false prophet is not necessarily a person who gives a wrong word. Balaam was called a false prophet, and he gave a correct word. It was his wrong motivation that was the problem.

In the New Testament, prophecy is clearly defined as something that needs to be judged and tested.[64]

> *Do not treat prophecies with contempt but **test** them all; hold on to what is good.*
>
> 1 Thessalonians 5:20-21, emphasis added

Why would you need to judge and test prophecy if all of it was perfect? Chapter thirteen of the book of First Corinthians tells us that each one of us knows in part and prophesies in part.[65] Here in Thessalonians, the Scripture tells us to hold on to the part that is good. All of these Scriptures are referring to the partial nature of prophecy, and partial information leaves room for errors. That is why healthy prophetic communities are so important. We cover one another and encourage one another to stay on track.

Internalization of New Concepts

Recently, I was studying the process whereby new concepts become an accepted norm within society. This process is called internalization. Internalization is the spiritual, psychological, and sociological process whereby an external concept or value becomes internal. It's the process where a new idea becomes an established concept within a community, or in this case, a prophetic company.

The general stages of internalization are as follows:

1. The new idea or concept is introduced, modeled, or conceived.

---

[64] 1 Cor. 14:29.

[65] 1 Cor. 13:9.

2. The new idea is verified as credible through research or practice.

3. The new idea is challenged, and conflicting ideas are presented.

4. The new idea or concept is accepted by the community.

Resistance training relates directly to the internalization process. Notice that conflict and challenge are a healthy part of the internalization process. When we see promises, commands, or concepts in the Bible that are currently not part of our normal practice, we have a responsibility to internalize them.

A person who attempts words of knowledge three times without getting any of the answers right might assume, "Well, this just isn't my gift. I'm no good at this." That judgment statement closes the gate of faith through which the gift or grace must pass. Even if the person has a measure of that gift or grace, it will be choked out by a beggarly personal expectation of what is possible. Potentially, this negative self-judgment could release the paralyzing lies of personal Cessationism and Exceptionism in formative stages.

The cure for wrong self-judgments is an atmosphere that encourages the conflict and celebrates the tension between potential and actual. We applaud anyone who is pursuing spiritual gifts in love and faith regardless of the outcome. Without welcoming and celebrating risk and potential failure, new ideas (or the restoration of old ones) is not possible. If we see conflicting feelings, ideas, and experiences as a normal part of internalizing a new concept, then we can press through to make our level of experience match the Bible rather than dumbing down the Bible to match our current level of experience. I discovered that one cannot over-emphasize how important conflict is to the building of prophetic community because it is such a healthy part of internalizing something new.

Rejection and Persecution

Rejection and persecution from external sources is also a healthy part of the internalization process. When you share a prophetic word and it doesn't go well or isn't well received, you have an opportunity to either make a judgment that closes the door or to make a fresh determination to continue. We don't encourage prophetic communities where people thrive off of rejection as if it is a validation of their spirituality, but we also don't deny that rejection and persecution are important contributors to the establishing of new values and ideals.

As I shared in an earlier chapter, Vilification is one of the ways that the supernatural life was quenched in other generations. Personal Vilification, where we question in an unhealthy way whether we are hearing from God or not, can keep us from living out the fullness that Christ died to release to us. We end up living for less than what He desires.

The Three Time Zones

Now that I have shared a little bit about how we have trained concerning the word of knowledge and perceptions of the past, I will share about the two remaining time zones: the present and the future. Present prophecy, or words of insight, are important for establishing healthy prophetic communities. One of the hindrances I have struggled with in my own prophetic journey is a concept I call anachronistic living. An anachronism is anything out of its proper time, e.g., spotting a mobile phone in the pocket of a character starring in an 1860s western. In prophecy, anachronisms are characterized by a tendency to view the future as a greater reality than the present.

Let me share an example of how anachronistic tendencies have plagued me. When I look at a person, I often do not see them as they currently are but rather through a prophetic lens of their future potential. Their potential shines so bright to me that it often overshadows their current struggles and limitations. If I put that person into a place of authority or responsibility that equals their potential rather than their actual current skill set, they will inevitably fail. This causes hurt both on their part—the pain of failing, and on mine—the pain of something not getting done right or at all. For years I mistakenly put people in the right place at the wrong time because I didn't recognize this anachronistic struggle.

Overcoming Anachronistic Challenges

That the future can seem more real than the present is a common limitation for prophetic people. Undiscerned, this perception leads to all kinds of frustration and hurt and can cause a rift between prophetic people and leadership. An anachronistic struggle within the local church can look much like the following scenario. The prophetic church member sees a potential for the church that feels like it should happen right now. The church leaders are not seeing the same future or are preoccupied with the tyranny of the urgent. The prophetic person becomes frustrated that the church is not moving towards its greater destiny. The church leadership is frustrated that the prophetic person doesn't seem to be able to engage in the current practical needs of the church. The result of these two differing viewpoints can be a perfect storm.

It can happen at home too. The prophet comes home from an exhilarating time of prophesying into the lives of individuals and plops down on the couch. Meanwhile, he can't see that the trash needs to be taken out and the lawn needs to be mowed. Resentment can build up in the heart of loved ones if the prophet doesn't learn to also see in real time. Balanced prophetic communities value and embrace the responsibility of real-life and real-time perceptions.

I have found anachronistic tendencies in many prophetic artists and songwriters as well. A prophetic songwriter will often compose songs that are three to five years ahead of where the church currently is. That is why when you look at the CCLI listing of songs that are currently being sung around the world, you will find that the average song on the list is three to five years old. This lag between when a song is written and when it becomes popular is not necessarily because the church is slow in adapting to change, but rather because prophetic people tend to be forerunners who are three to five years ahead of where the rest of the church is at.

The Right Word in the Right Time

For this reason, we must understand that every prophetic revelation or perception must await its appointed time.[66] If you present a song or word in the wrong season, it won't be received well. The word is not wrong; it is the season that is mismatched. That's why the Scripture says that a word in its season is like apples of gold in a setting of silver.[67] The gold represents the divine; the apple is the word or revelation; the silver represents redemption, and the socket is the proper time and place. Therefore, we should look for the redemptive timing and setting for our "apples of gold" and not pout or complain when a word out of season is not duly honored.

That's why prophetic communities need to learn to deal with real-time perceptions. They need to train their gifts to work here and now and partner with leadership in what is currently going on. We need prophetic reformers not protesters. A basic difference between protesters and reformers is that protesters stay outside of the process and system complaining about what is wrong. Reformers are willing to climb inside of a system and respect and honor what is good about where it is at currently. Reformers serve and partner to retain what is currently valuable as they assist in moving the church or organization forward toward its more desirable future.

Embracing the Future

This is not to say that we should not train in prophesying towards the future. As we saw in early chapters, predictive prophecy makes up a significant portion of the biblical text. The real issue in predictive prophecy is accountability. There are myriads of internet prophets making constant disaster predictions with no accountability for when things do or don't come true. Of course, if you wait long enough, natural disasters have a cycle and weather tragedies will eventually occur.

---

[66] Hab. 2:2-3.

[67] Prov. 25:11, NASB.

Some prophets take the occurrence of these tragedies as validations for their prophetic ministry. Any prophet who feels vindicated through tragedy and loss of life does not know what spirit they are of.[68] We need to train prophetic companies to speak to our prophetic future with hope and accountability.

In our monthly trainings, we ask our prophetic company to practice making predictions in a specific sphere which they believe will come true over the following thirty days. Students write down their predictions, sign it, and place it in a sealed envelope. In the following month's training, we open the envelopes and evaluate our accuracy.

For instance, in 2014, Northern California was facing the third year of a historically severe drought. In fact, 2013 was the driest year on record since the state began measuring rainfall in 1849 and, according to the width of old tree rings, the driest in 500 years.[69] Many people prayed for rain, but we felt like the Lord was calling us to speak prophetically to the rain. I asked our students to tell me what day it would rain and how much. On November 21, 2014, with hardly a drop of rain since the typical rainy season began, thirteen of our prophetic company predicted a record rainfall in the month of December. On December 12, 2014, the National Weather Service for San Francisco and Monterey Bay Area posted to their Twitter account: "Yesterday's rain total of 3.23 inches in San Jose. It's the wettest December day ever recorded at the site. Records back to 1893."[70] One of our students predicted a near exact amount of rain: "Record rainfall 2.8 inches within a 24-hour period." According to weatherspark.com: "The day with the largest quantity of precipitation in Vacaville, California, during 2014 was Thursday, December 11. That day saw 2.844 of liquid precipitation, compared to a median value of 0.196."[71] Truly, a record rainfall had occurred within the predicted time frame and to the prophesied amount during a severe drought!

---

[68] Luke 9:55.

[69] huffingtonpost.com/2014/01/30/california-drought-effects-500-years

[70] twitter.com/NWSBayArea/status/543443224249913344

[71] weatherspark.com/history/31880/2014/vacaville-california

Predictive prophecy is also part of our life skill training. While focusing on the mountain of education, we did word of knowledge drills naming individuals' school facts; we did insight words over our current school board president; we did prediction drills concerning the outcome of our local school board elections. There were eleven candidates and four winners. Team members were asked to predict the four winners, the percentage by which they would win, and the overall popular vote. Though no one predicted all of this information perfectly, many definitely defied the law of probabilities and statistics by predicting all four winners and the general range of victory percentages. Even when we don't get answers perfectly right, our prophetic company is not easily frustrated or disappointed with our results. We know that if we keep exercising and practicing, we will grow in grace, knowledge, and faith.

As a prophetic company, we have embraced the fact that maturity comes through practice. By providing a safe, loving, and accountable environment for practice, we are training a prophetic community who is not afraid to partner with Heaven for the revelation or causation of future events. Though there is still much spiritual ground to take in the area of predictive prophecy, as a community, we are pursuing the biblical mandate to eagerly desire greater spiritual gifts.[72]

In the final chapter, I will share some of the ways we are exploring advanced prophetic training.

---

[72] 1 Cor. 12:31; 14:1.

12

Advancing Prophetic Company

Two of the many things I enjoy in life are family holidays and studying revival history. One year around the Christmas season, I was combining two of my favorite things by doing some research on Saint Nicholas. Nicholas' status as the "patron saint of children" reportedly came from his acts of generosity to the poor and varied accounts of his rescuing kidnapped children using the gift of word of knowledge. He essentially broke up a child slavery ring operating in his day. As I read the inspiring accounts of Nicholas' life, my heart was drawn to a mental image of the pictures of missing children that line the exits of our large department stores in America. According to the National Center for Missing and Exploited Children, approximately 800,000 children are reported missing each year in the United States. That's roughly 2,000 per day.

Finding Missing Children

I began to wonder if we could use the perceptions of our prophetic company to serve families with missing children. I started an experiment in one of our monthly trainings by printing posters I found on the internet of missing children from our area. I looked particularly for posters that offered a bit of backstory giving some of the details of the child's abduction. We divided the class into teams and gave each team a poster. A prophetic coach facilitated each of the teams. The coaches printed out a sheet of specific details or the backstory regarding the abduction, but they were asked to keep this information to themselves. The only clues the team members were given were the name and picture of the child.

Next, we asked team members to listen for a word of knowledge revealing any information regarding the child's abduction. In this way, coaches could check the accuracy of the team's perceptions using the backstory information they had been provided along with the poster. The idea here is that if the word of knowledge information is on track, we knew we were hearing clearly from the Lord and had the confidence to venture into seeking unknown information about the abduction. Students first worked independently within the team to get information and perceptions from the Lord. Then the group would come together and share their impressions. Perceptions that were similar to other student's impressions were treated with a higher priority. In this exercise, one of our teams perceived accurately the make, model, and color of the car that abducted a child as well as the names of the two suspects involved. With the ability to verify these facts through what I had downloaded from the missing children website, our faith and encouragement rose to another level.

The accuracy of these words of knowledge gave us confidence to direct our perceptions toward whether the child was living or deceased. The team felt by the Spirit of the Lord that the little girl was still alive. We asked God for pictures and perceptions of where the child was being held and wisdom on how she might be rescued or escape. As it was our first attempt, we didn't know more to do than just declare her freedom into the atmosphere. Three days later, this little girl who had been missing for nearly three years was found and restored to her family. In the months that followed, one of our prophet leaders had perceptions that aligned with locating two other missing children.

As word of these testimonies circulated, parents, grandparents, and even a police officer approached our prophetic company about helping to find missing and exploited children in our region. I can't adequately express what this did to my heart personally. Several years earlier, I was merely asking the question, "What does a prophetic company look like?" Now, I was living in the budding reality of a prophetic company that could serve the community in ways I had never even dreamed were possible. This confirmed my theory that prophecy is not meant to be simply a ministry skill, but a life skill to serve every sphere of society.

Reviewing Prophetic Company

Before we move into exploring other advanced areas of prophetic pursuit, I'd like to review some of our discoveries of what a prophetic company can look like. First of all, in a prophetic company, it is believed that everyone can prophesy. A prophetic company fulfills the dream of God that every son and daughter prophesy by the outpouring of His Holy Spirit. A prophetic company understands that though everyone can prophesy, not everyone prophesies the same way. This is why our prophetic community recognizes five spokes that contribute to the prophetic atmosphere. These spokes are team members, coaches, seers and mystics, prophets, and presbyters.

Next, we recognize that a prophetic company acts on its prophetic words. We train individuals how to judge, sort, and process prophetic words in the company of loved ones and leaders. Our community is determined to activate, strategize, and mobilize prophetic words that have been judged to be from God. We partner with Heaven to agree with our words, align ourselves with the word's potential and conditions, and begin to appropriate the favor, authority, and identity we draw from processing our words.

Finally, a prophetic company is a people who believe in prophetic diversity. Diversity is not only acknowledged, it is celebrated and pursued. We train our prophetic company in the many different ways that prophetic perceptions can be perceived and delivered. We celebrate seers, hearers, feelers, perceivers, and the diverse manners of operation or workings of the gifts. We seek out the different ways that prophecy can be delivered verbally, written, given, acted out, and displayed. The three dimensional nature of our gifts is embraced. Prophetic builders, messengers, advancers, strategists, refiners, watchmen, reformers, counselors, inventors, writers, intercessors, artists, musicians, and all manner of prophetic applications are valued in the prophetic company.

Advancing the Prophetic

We discovered that prophetic training should be intentional, proactive, and adventurous. Our beginners focus on the different ways of perceiving the voice of God and delivering a prophetic word. Intermediate levels explore prophecy as a life skill and practice prophesying from the three time zones of past, present, and future perceptions.

With this established, we now had to ask what does advanced prophetic training look like?

One of the goals of our intermediate training was to expose team members to various spheres of influence to find the places where their gifts and graces most come alive. As we mentioned in earlier chapters, this would indicate a metron, or sphere of influence. Advanced training starts with someone who has discovered their primary sphere of influence. A quick word of caution: our metron does not limit where we can prophesy or who we can minister too; it only defines where our grace seems to most consistently abound. This sphere of influence forms a "sweet spot" for a person's prophetic gift where he or she tends to manifest greater authority, accuracy, and ease.

Focused Prophetic

As a person discovers the dimensions of his prophetic gift and calling, he is able to focus the training from the general to the specific. While beginner and intermediate training focuses on discovering the variety of prophetic options that are available to us, advanced training centers around a primary sphere of influence. Advanced training is a season of specialization. Currently at The Mission, we reserve advanced training for those who believe they have the call to the office of prophet.

One of our prophets, Keith Ferrante, runs a two-year School of Emerging Prophets. The school involves mentoring, discipling, teaching, training, activation, and fieldwork. One of its roles is to help those called to the prophetic office discern and train for their specific spheres of influence. Many of those who attend the school come to realize that they don't have the call to the office of prophet but rather, enjoy a higher-level of prophetic gifting. Those who do have the call to the office are asked to formulate a project that advances prophetic ministry within their sphere of influence.[73]

Prophetic Journaling

I won't spend more time here talking about our advanced school because it may not necessarily relate to the reader's community. I will, however, share some ways that I believe a person who doesn't have access to a school like this can train themselves on an advanced level.

For the one who believes he has the call of a prophet, I first recommend beginning a prophet's journal in the area of your sphere of influence. In the journal, record prophetic perceptions for people within your target audience. Date the prophecies and watch for the fulfillment. When prophecies come true or are verified, record the date of confirmation along with any documentation.

For instance, if you believe you are called to the mountain of government, choose a city leader, state leader, national leader, and international leader to prophesy over. At least three times a week, record in your journal past, present, and future impressions over these leaders. Prophetic perceptions could cover areas like family, business, relationships, spiritual encounters, obstacles, and events. Then watch

---

[73] Keith Ferrante is currently setting up his School of Emerging Prophets online.

media resources and/or do research regarding your prophetic targets to test the accuracy of your words. I recommend that you as an emerging prophet resist the urge to send any of these prophecies to the individual government leaders until you have trained at least two to three years.

Journaling gives the prophet-in-training the opportunity to build the measure of faith needed to prophesy over governmental leaders. By knowing your accuracy level, your confidence and faith are built up. Journaling over several years will also help you discover what I would call your anachronistic differential, meaning the average length of time between when you prophesy something and its fulfillment. Much wisdom comes from retrospective reflection. When you see a major prophecy come true, then you can reflect back and ask yourself, "How did this impression differ from others? How did it feel? Was it stronger? More clear? Did it come in a different way than an average perception?" Questions like these help you recognize the general times and seasons associated with your prophetic perceptions. You can come to know the average fulfillment of a word when you deliver it and then put an accurate timestamp on the word. You will be able to accurately say things like, "I feel like this speaks to your current season," or "this is something not far off," or "in a season far from now." Helping people to know the times and seasons of words even as they are delivered reduces the frustration that comes from assuming all words are intended to happen now. This level of information also helps the receiver in prophetic processing.

Journaling may also reveal when one might not have a sustained grace for the area they feel called to. If a person loses interest in his journaling project, then he probably doesn't have an office call to that field, or at least it's not time to proactively pursue this area. It doesn't mean that the person will never have the call, but it may mean that the person is out of season with taking that office.

The Law of Attraction

Keeping a prophetic journal can also engage a sort of law of attraction. What you honor and respect, you are more likely to attract.

Training for something you believe you are called to is a demonstration of active faith that attracts the favor of God. Many people believe things about themselves and their calling but never move towards it. I don't consider these beliefs faith but rather spiritual fantasies. You only truly believe what you are willing to act on. Faith that hits your feet—that takes action—is the kind of faith that is a catalyst for greater God-encounters and supernatural appointments.

We have an amazing intercessor in our prophetic company who felt a call to pray prophetically for a well-known movie star. This was not a schoolgirl crush, but a real burden of the heart. For many years, she would write down the impressions she had about this man's life, family, career, and faith. One day, she and a friend heard that the movie star was shooting a film near their home city. They went on location and stood behind the roped-off area watching the film being shot. At one point, the movie star looked at the fans gathered behind the perimeter and made eye contact with our intercessor. Their eyes locked for a moment in such a way that he sent someone to bring her onto the set.

He asked, "Do I know you? You look familiar."

"No," she replied "But I know you. I've been praying for you for years." Then she shared a word of the Lord over his life that she had been crafting for many years. The movie star was deeply touched, and it is surely a moment neither one will ever forget. There is a spiritual law of attraction that can be summed up in the idea that you attract what you demonstrate active faith for.

Dreaming Forward

There is a wonderful passage found in the book of First Corinthians that encourages us to dream forward in the area of advanced prophetic training. It says, "What no eye has seen, what no ear has heard, and what no human mind has conceived—the things God has prepared for those who love him—these are the things God has revealed to us by his Spirit."[74]

---

[74] 1 Cor. 2:9b-10.

It's time to use our prophetic grace and divine union to dream forward what is possible in prophetic realms. There is not a single path or pattern to follow. The Father is watching for prophetic companies eagerly pursuing prophecy and activating their faith in new ways that He can pour out His revelations upon. There are new wineskins emerging to hold this fresh wine of prophetic grace poured out on every son and daughter.

In my spirit, I see prophetic teams focused on ending droughts with prophetic acts and declarations, prophetic companies who partner with medical entities to prophetically diagnose and cure diseases, and teams who use prophetic declarations to regularly raise the dead. I see prophetic counselors to governors and kings as well as parenting seminars presenting prophetic revelations of new strategies to parent children. I see prophetic business consultants predicting financial trends and visioneering new markets and structures. The possibilities are literally endless with the dimensionality of our gifts and spheres. These discoveries of new ways to train in the prophetic are only waiting for those who will take the time to build prophetic companies that will dream forward with God.

A Call to Build

Concerning the prophetic company at The Mission, let me be clear—I'm not proposing in this book that you adopt our five prophetic spokes, our three methods of training, or our three definitions of prophetic company. I am, however, calling you to discover and build your own unique prophetic company.

Let me ask you the question that the prophet asked me so many years ago, "Are you a prophetic company or do you just love prophecy?"

Prophetic companies are a biblical and historical response to the dream of God's heart that every son and daughter would truly know the heart, the mind, and the thoughts of their heavenly Father. The worst thing you could do right now is nothing, but a close second would be impulsively appointing the most prophetically gifted people in your community into a structure that doesn't fit your calling, values, or potential outcome.

Instead, I recommend that you start building prophetic company by evaluating your strengths and your weaknesses. I ask you to consider these questions.

- What do you have already in your midst as raw material for building prophetic company?

- What pieces are most lacking?

- How many people in your community currently function with at least a beginner level of prophetic grace?

- Do you have a prophet—or multiple prophets—in your community?

- What sphere of influence or metron does your prophetic office serve?

- Do you have a clear protocol for how the prophetic operates within your community?

- Do you have prophetic training programs in place?

- How are the people skills within your prophetic company?

- What are the greatest challenges facing you in building a local prophetic company?

By asking great questions like these and by evaluating your prophetic resources, you can begin to discover how to build prophetic company in your community.

Your journey may parallel ours in some ways or it may look entirely different based upon your own resources, your spheres of influence, and your goals. The important thing is that you start: start asking questions, start evaluating resources, start dreaming what the people of a prophetic company could accomplish together.

Partnering with Leaders

Another important step to building prophetic company is partnering with other five-fold leaders. Prophetic company should not be built only by those involved in the prophetic. The foundation of the church is built upon apostles and prophets.[75] The apostolic grace is really helpful in establishing vision and direction. The teacher gift helps keep prophetic impressions biblical and sound. Pastors release grace to love and care for one another which has been a huge missing piece to the puzzle of prophetic company. Evangelists keep us focused on a kingdom expression of prophecy that looks out upon the needs of a lost world rather than just a church-focused "bless me" club. To build healthy prophetic company, you will need the grace of all the five-fold offices. You may not have access to someone who functions in each of the five-fold offices within your local community, but you can still seek out an expression of that grace within your prophetic company.

I also love sitting down with business leaders, government leaders, teachers, and parents to ask them what kind of prophetic information and services are helpful. For instance, our police department informed me that they wanted no background information, only "actionable data." In other words, they didn't care how we got the information or what the impressions were, they only wanted a few bits of specific bullet-point information that an officer or detective could take immediate action on. The information we received from that interview was super helpful in shaping how we train our prophetic community. Each prophetic sphere will have a different set of protocols for how they will operate. These protocols are a result of the vision, values, and desired outcome of the prophetic ministry within that sphere.

Our interviews with businessmen revealed that prophetic questions were as helpful as prophetic declarations. Consultants ask great questions. This helped us train prophetic listeners not just speakers. A friend of mine trained a small portion of their prophetic company to minister in the mountain of government. They learned proper protocol for conduct and conversations with government leaders from interviewing someone who worked in government security. Many of

---

[75] Eph. 2:2.

the parameters for how we train and what our targets are came from interviews like these. Find out what those you want to serve are really looking for, and then train for their needs. In this way, you will not find yourself answering questions no one is asking.

Building with Prayer

Perhaps it goes without saying, but prophetic company should also be built upon a foundation of prayer. I feel that partnering with prayer leaders helps keep prophecy a matter of the heart and not just a strategy from the head. I talked a lot in this book about self-initiated training, stirring your gift, and moving God, but in the end, we joyously acknowledge the reality that the greatest partnership must always be surrendering to the Holy Spirit. After all, prophecy is truly a matter of hearing, seeing, feeling, or perceiving what He is doing and then acting on it.

Prophecy must be more than methodology; it must ever be a tool for tapping into the abundant grace of God. Our structure and methods are not the river; they are only the banks that help us channel and harness the strength of what God is doing. If we get too far from prayer and intimacy, we may find ourselves with a form of godliness that has no real power.[76]

One of the dangers of a strong prophetic structure is that gifts can operate outside of intimate relationship. We can learn the ways of prophecy without having the true heart of prophecy. This is one of the warnings of the love chapter.

> *If I have the gift of prophecy and can fathom all mysteries and knowledge, and if I have a faith that can move mountains, but do not have love, I am nothing.*

> 1 Corinthians 13:2

---

[76] 2 Tim. 3:5.

Never let the knowledge of how prophecy works take you away from the heart of *why* it works. Gifts are irrevocable graces given by the most loving and generous being in the universe. God trusts us with His amazing manifestations of power and only asks that we keep them within the boundaries of love. Without God's presence, His power has no redemptive context. We want all displays of His power to give Him glory, and honor, and power forever and ever.

The Prophetic Unction

So, here we are, standing ankle deep in the waters of the greatest prophetic movement in history. Never before have so many believers acted on the prophetic grace poured out on all flesh. What will we do with this entrustment? How will we steward this amazing grace? If God's dream was to truly fill every son and daughter with a prophetic unction and the fullness of God, how can we best partner with His dream? I believe it is time for prophetic companies to arise throughout the earth. These companies will possess different flavors, structures, and missions, but each one will make a significant contribution to demonstrating life "on earth as it is in heaven."[77]

An army is rising. A great wind is blowing. In the mission of building prophetic company, I hear the Lord calling, "Who will go for Me, and whom shall I send?" It only takes a willing heart and a humble, "Here am I, send me."[78]

May God bless and increase all those who respond.

---

[77] Matt. 6:10.

[78] Isa. 6:8.

About the Author

Dan McCollam travels internationally as a prophetic speaker and trainer. He strategizes with churches and individuals to create prophetic cultures in which everyone can hear God, activate and mobilize their prophetic words, and express their own unique prophetic diversity.

Dan has developed many resources that offer a fresh perspective on the prophetic, supernatural kingdom life, biblical character, and spiritual gifting. He is well-known as a great friend of the Holy Spirit and one who carries and imparts wisdom, revelation, and breakthrough.

Dan serves on the teaching faculty of Bethel School of the Prophets and the Bethel School of Worship, in Redding, California. Along with his wife, Regina, Dan serves on the leadership team at his home church, The Mission, in Vacaville, California, and is a director of MissionU, a school of supernatural ministry, also in Vacaville.

Sounds of the Nations

After serving as a worship leader for 20 years and releasing kingdom worshipers locally, regionally, and globally on countless mission trips to nations around the world, Dan became troubled over the westernization of worship in the majority of churches in which he ministered. Indigenous sounds had often been labeled sinful by church leadership. Since the sounds of every tribe and nation are heard in Heaven, becoming an agent in restoring the stolen authentic expressions of worship became a driving passion for Dan, and Sounds of the Nations was born.

As international director of Sounds of the Nations, Dan trains indigenous peoples to write and record worship songs using their own ethnic sounds, styles, languages, and instruments.

For more information about Sounds of the Nations, contact us by email: SOTNtraining@gmail.com.

Resources

Other books and resource material by Dan McCollam

BASIC TRAINING FOR PROPHETIC ACTIVATION (book)

This powerful book unearths several simple tools that will fan into flame the gift of God that is in you. It is full of practical insights where you will learn: the prophetic nature of a name; how your five senses can be activated by Holy Spirit to receive heavenly insight; how to bring people into the kingdom with the gift of prophecy; how to process your own prophetic words for greater empowerment.

SPIRITUAL GIFTS (audio set)

What does passionately pursuing these gifts of the Spirit look like in everyday life? Author and teacher Dan McCollam encourages the red-hot burning pursuit of biblical Christianity as he instructs powerful and practical ways to explore, express, and pursue the spiritual gifts described in 1 Corinthians 12:7-11.

IMPARTATION (audio set)

IMPARTATION through the laying on of hands is a fundamental teaching of the New Testament church. In this two-part series, Dan McCollam explores and activates five types of impartation: distributed, apprehended, residual, atmospheric, and relational.

THE THREE-DIMENSIONAL NATURE OF SPIRITUAL GIFTS
(Audio set)

Based on 1 Corinthians 12:4-6, this teaching brings an understanding of the differing gifts, differing administrations and differing operations. Embracing the three-dimensional nature of spiritual gifts unlocks a greater freedom and operation of those gifts in the life of the believer.

MY SUPER POWERS (Children's Books)

Volume One
Word of Wisdom
Word of Knowledge
Gift of Faith

Volume Two
Gifts of Healing
Working of Miracles
Gift of Prophecy

Volume Three
Gift of Discernment
Gift of Tongues
Interpretation of Tongues

Available at store.imissionchurch.com and Amazon.com

MY SUPER POWERS is a series of children's books based on the nine gifts of the Holy Spirit mentioned in 1 Corinthians 12:8-9. Children don't receive a pint-sized Holy Spirit but all the fullness of God the same as any adult. These stories are intended to show how children can operate in the gifts of the Spirit at an early age.

All resources are available at:

store.imissionchurch.com